UNDERSTANDING MOURNING

A Guide For Those Who Grieve

Glen W. Davidson

AUGSBURG PUBLISHING HOUSE • MINNEAPOLIS

Blessed are those who mourn,
for they shall be comforted.
—Matthew 5:4

UNDERSTANDING MOURNING
A Guide for Those Who Grieve

Copyright © 1984 Augsburg Publishing House

Scripture quotations unless otherwise noted are from the Revised Standard Version of the Bible, copyright 1946, 1952, and 1971 by the Division of Christian Education of the National Council of Churches.

Library of Congress Cataloging in Publication Data

Davidson, Glen W.
  UNDERSTANDING MOURNING

  Bibliography: p. 102
  1. Bereavement—Psychological aspects.   I. Title.
BF575.G7D38   1984   155.9'37   84-14527
ISBN 0-8066-2080-3

Manufactured in the U.S.A.   APH 10-6805

                          14   15   16   17   18

Contents

Preface

Understanding mourning is no small task. It requires not only understanding how mourners grieve, how they react to change, and how physical and emotional functioning may become erratic—but it requires this understanding at a time when a person's usual perceptions, reasoning abilities, and ways of interpreting reality are distorted. Under the stress of loss, mourners may not see and hear accurately or be able to think clearly. Mourners are highly vulnerable, as much to events of their own making as to events forced upon them, as much to the consequences of their own feelings as to the desires of others.

This book is written for the mourner. The book begins where many mourners begin—at the point of crisis. The three case histories in Chapter 1 show how losses of a spouse, child, relative, or friend are intensely personal but also have profound impact on others as well. All personal stories in this book are based on actual experiences of mourners. Names and identifying features have been changed in order to protect confidentiality.

These experiences of mourning are interpreted from the perspective of a research project I began in 1967 while on the faculty of the University of Chicago. I had studied the work done by the British psychiatrists John Bowlby and Colin Murray Parkes, and I was eager to see if their conclusions about the changing characteristics of mourning would hold true in North America as well.[1] Over a period of 10 years, I followed 1200 adult mourners in order to record as accurately as possible their common experiences.

The idea of *mourning* is extremely old and has been preserved in two of humanity's most ancient languages. The root meaning in Sanskrit is "to remember" and in Greek is "to care." Mourning is an emotion that results from the universal experience of loss. I use the word to mean the way in which mourners adapt from what *was* to what *is*. To grieve (to be burdened by sorrow) and to be bereaved (to be robbed of someone or something precious) are part of—but only part of—the mourning process. Mourning is a process that takes you on the journey from where you were before loss to where you will be as you struggle to adapt to change in your life.

Each individual experiences loss in intensely personal ways. Severed personal relationships are some of the most painful consequences of death. Because their lives have been disrupted, mourners are often disoriented. Mourning is a process of recovering orientation—becoming involved once again in human relationships. As you read this book, do not try to imitate the experiences of others, but let their struggles help guide you in overcoming your own disorientation.

Understanding Mourning is a companion volume to *Living with Dying*, first published in 1975. In that work I focused on how family, friends, and members of the helping professions can better understand the emotional and spiritual needs of those who are dying. *Understanding Mourning* focuses on the needs of the survivors of loss. It is intended to help mourners cope with the universal but personally painful experience of loss.

I owe a special word of thanks for the many people who have encouraged me to write for, as well as about, mourners. In particular I wish to thank my dean, Richard H. Moy, M.D., who over the years has provided a highly stimulating context not only for completing my study but also for pursuing its implications; to my colleagues in the departments of Medical

Humanities and Psychiatry, who have regularly challenged me to define what I am doing; to Linda Keldermans, editorial assistant, Lynne Cleverdon, administrative assistant, and Helen Melnyk, secretary, who have very patiently helped with the manuscript; to the Southern Illinois University School of Medicine Library staff for help with references, and the Biomedical Communications artists for preparing the figures; to my editors, who have guided this book with such caring assurance; and finally to Shirlee Proctor Davidson, R.N., who has not only been my most helpful critic but my most faithful companion through our own losses.

This is a book for mourners about the work of overcoming the disorientation that follows loss of a loved one. It is testimony of both the pain of loss and the gift of new life.

GLEN W. DAVIDSON

1

Telling Your Story

If left to their own designs, most people would ignore mourning, just as
they try to ignore other disagreeable experiences in life. Once
loss occurs—and it happens to everyone at some time—
mourning is not commonly discussed, except for those una-
voidable aspects that cannot be suppressed. This book is directed to those who are normal, based on research into what
is normal. Normal people suffer and normal people mourn.

Marge's Story

Loss of a spouse is a common experience, because few couples die simultaneously. Throughout their years together,
however, many couples do not discuss what the survivor can
expect financially or socially, let alone emotionally and spiritually. Marge's experience is common. Married for 40 years,
she had helped put her husband Sam through college, raised
three children, worked as a homemaker, and was widowed
at 62. Sam expected to retire at 65 and had planned that he
and Marge would retire to Florida to enjoy their sunset years
playing in the warm climate with friends their own age. Sam's

pension and Social Security would provide modest financial security.

Sam began to feel ill several years before he would have retired. At first his symptoms were vague, but they were diagnosed eventually as a fast-growing cancer. He was able to continue working sporadically for another six months. Sam spent his last days under the care of the local hospice team, which made it possible for Marge to care for him at home. It was there that he died. Because they were relatively young, Sam and Marge had wanted the doctors to "do everything possible," but as successive treatments proved ineffective, they were forced to consider a different future.

Despite the events that forced Marge to begin making plans for being alone, the sense of foreboding she had before Sam's death, and the long lonely nights in which she tried to prepare herself for the inevitable, Sam's death was a shock to her. She reported: "I was prepared, I thought, and then when he died, I found that I wasn't prepared at all. I felt overwhelmed and alone. I simply didn't want to face the future by myself."

Linda and Gordon's Story

Loss of a child is uncommon today. Prenatal care, high-risk nurseries, and sophisticated technology have all reduced the rate of infant mortality. But all the successes of science did not spare Linda and Gordon. Their son died shortly after birth, an event unexpected both by them and their obstetrician.

Linda has difficulty remembering the details of her baby's birth and death. She remembers vividly, though, how she was made to feel. She felt like a failure.

Linda did not see her son, either living or dead. He was whisked away to a high-risk nursery. She was moved to the gynecology service away from the nursery area. Few people spoke to her, and those who did avoided mentioning the baby. Her physician gave her medication to stop lactation.

Gordon arranged a private funeral while Linda was still in the hospital. Together with his mother, they had the nursery furniture stored away and had even repainted the room, "so she wouldn't be reminded of the baby" when she came home.

"It was unreal," Linda explained. "I thought I had gone to the hospital to have a baby. When I came home, everyone seemed in a conspiracy to suggest that it had never happened. After a while I even began to doubt that I had been pregnant."

Erica and Warren's Story

There was no conspiracy of silence for Erica and Warren. The death of their 19-year-old son was headline news. Everyone in town talked about the accident in which a prominent citizen, driving a car while under the influence of alcohol, ran the youth and his motorcycle off the road. Their son was fatally injured and pronounced dead at the hospital emergency room.

It was difficult to tell who was most angry—Warren or the community at large. In public Warren kept himself "under control." In private all he could think about was revenge. In the past Warren had had some unpleasant business with the driver of the car. So had many others in town. The driver had a recognized problem with alcohol and even had his driver's license suspended for a time. He tended to be "a wheeler-dealer," and, in Warren's words, "contributed nothing positive to the community." Warren's son had been a star athlete in high school, active in the church youth group, affable, and well-liked.

Erica and Warren's pastor commented that the funeral was the most difficult of his ministry. The pastor found doubts about God crowding out any notion of love and justice. He confessed to the congregation that he was at the funeral as a fellow mourner, confused and frustrated, and together they must "wait on the mercies of Almighty God."

The funeral would have been a "healing experience," according to Erica, except that the driver of the car came "drunk and blubbering." Warren called the man a murderer. Everyone was terribly upset. The funeral director described the scene as a nightmare. Rather than a time to pull the community together for emotional support, the funeral became the occasion for further isolation as the emotions of anger and embarrassment dominated the scene.

Your Story

These are only three of the thousands of stories that could be shared by mourners. Although they are not your story, they relate the grief of real people. Yet the most important story is *your own* story of mourning. Only in the telling of your story can you recover the most important thing in your life—your basic life orientation. This is more important than your feelings about the person you lost, your concerns about what others think, or your business affairs.

That which is most important is what I call *orientation*. When we experience a loss, particularly through death, it is natural to become disoriented. From a medical perspective, mourners become *dysfunctional*, which means that day-to-day health needs are not handled as competently as before the loss. From a psychological perspective, mourners become confused, distracted, and preoccupied, so that decision making is difficult. From a theological perspective, mourners become distrustful because they must rethink not only who or what can be trusted, but whether one can trust at all.

Relationships to other people, to the physical surroundings in which one lives, and to the time context in which activities take place are basic aspects of orientation. Orientation is so basic that many people are not aware of it until it is compromised or absent. Child psychologists have found that even newborn babies have a basic orientation to their mothers, probably based on the sounds of the mother's voice and other sensations that each child came to know even while in the uterus. Normal growth and development is the maturing of orientation to person, place, and time.

The verb *to orient* means to face eastward, and refers to the European (and later, North American) tradition of measuring where one is in place and time by one's relationship to a fixed spot in the East. Many Christians, for example, worship regularly in churches that face toward Jerusalem. Muslims pray daily, bowing toward Mecca. It is natural to take our bearings from someone or something that is, if not fixed forever in the structure of the universe, at least outside or beyond us.

To be disoriented is to be lost. Everyone becomes disoriented momentarily every time something unexpected is encountered. Orientation is recovered quickly as individuals refer to a familiar person, place, or time. It is normal to measure what is new against what is known. Mental adjustments are made so quickly that people frequently fail to realize how often they go through processes of reorientation. That is, they fail to realize this until they encounter an experience to which they cannot readily adapt. For some people, the disorientation may be so profound that they feel—or are seen by others as—crazy. The disorientation most people feel after the loss of someone they love is frustrating. They find it difficult to think clearly, and often they feel a general malaise. From their perspective the world is in disarray. Subsequent disorientation becomes ever more frightening as they struggle to maintain normalcy. To be oriented once again becomes their most important goal in life.

Telling your story will be the most important thing for you to do as a mourner, because in the very act of telling it you are putting your life back together. By telling your story you will discover that your facts change, not because the facts themselves are changed but because your choice of what is important changes. You may discover that your initial impressions of what happened were incomplete or even inaccurate. The more unexpected the death, the more likely it is that initial impressions were wrong.

Warren found that as he told the story of losing his son over and over again, new facts came to light. Apparently his son was not forced off the road by the driver of the car, but, having taken a shortcut, had pulled into the lane of highway traffic from a side road. The driver of the car, his reflexes dulled by alcohol, failed to avoid hitting the motorcycle, and Warren's son was thrown into the culvert. The change of facts did not bring back his son, but Warren was able to reorient himself on the basis of what happened rather than on the basis of conjecture.

As you first tell your story, you will probably not be able to provide an ending. Some people try. They say things like, "This is God's will," or "It was meant to be." More unfortunate are those mourners who, in trying to tell their story, are given endings by other people who share "words of advice," give "testimony," or respond with clichés. Linda, for example, was told that she ought not mourn because she was young and could have another baby. Marge was told that she was old and had lived a full life. Erica and Warren were told that they should find comfort in the fact that their son had brought them so much pride. All these endings simply did not fit. Rather than helping these mourners become reoriented, such clichés only further disoriented them.

Telling the story of your loss over and over is more important than having a "right ending," at least for a while. In the telling, you are able to get the facts straight and distinguish reality from imagination. To change the metaphor, mourners must clear away the debris of their collapsed world in order to find the foundation on which to rebuild their lives—to recover their orientation. Telling your story over and over will be your most important task.

What happens if you cannot tell your story—if it's too horrible, too unimportant to others, or too imposing? The consequence is that you will remain disoriented. Although mourning draws out feelings of loneliness, it always has social dimensions. Without telling our story again and again to others, we find it nearly impossible to recover a sense of order.

The ancient Hebrews, the church Fathers, and modern re-searchers all seem to have identified something basic to hu-man nature when they have encouraged rituals that involve the telling of stories, particularly those stories that recall major changes in life. These changes affect everyone, and they in-clude changes of the seasons like winter and spring, changes of living conditions like harvests and plantings, and the changes of relationships like births, marriages, and deaths.

You will need to tell your story of loss and change again and again in order to get your facts straight, clarify how you are part of the facts, discover how your life has been changed by those facts, and finally to determine how you fit into the arrangement of the universe. Some people refer to these tasks in theological terms as they try to find how, even in their changed world, they fit into God's order.

What follows is not an attempt to tell you what your story is, or to instruct you in what you should tell, or even to urge you to conclude your story in a particular way. I give no formula for escaping the work of mourning. Instead I share what I have learned in order that you may gain the confidence necessary to tell your story in your own way and that you may have available what is known about mourning as you seek to recover your orientation to living. To mourn appro-priately is to tell your story effectively.

Before looking at ways you can tell your story, it is impor-tant to examine some common misunderstandings about mourning.

1. Mourning lasts from 48 hours to two weeks

After the Vietnam War, a journalist for a major Midwestern newspaper conducted a scientific poll in which he asked, "How long is it normal to mourn the loss of a loved one?" The overwhelming majority thought that individuals should be through mourning between 48 hours and two weeks after a death. This poll has been replicated a number of times with little variation in findings, regardless of the age or gender of the respondent, the region in which respondents live, or their educational level. In my own research, I have found that even physicians and nurses who work with mourners on a regular basis assume that mourning ought to be short. They become very concerned if the mourner exhibits characteristics of grief much beyond the first month. Even those who have experienced a personal loss expect that they ought to be over mourning much sooner than the facts confirm. When presented with the research findings that mourning takes much longer than they assumed, people often respond, "But I thought I was the only one that wasn't handling this appropriately."

Research into bereavement has made it clear that the mourning process is complex and the period of mourning lasts far longer than most people expect. In addition, many characteristics of bereavement are often not identified by the general public as being a part of mourning.

2. "Keep busy! Don't think!"

A second common misunderstanding is that the best way of handling grief is to keep busy and try to suppress thoughts about the deceased. Many mourners do indeed try to handle the disequilibrium and the disorientation of their grief by keeping busy. Mourners often change homes, communities, jobs, and even spouses. Others feel it is important to take long trips, to buy long-wanted items, to remarry quickly if widowed, or to have another pregnancy if they have lost a child.

Undoubtedly, considerable comfort is found in being able to keep one's hands occupied. It is an error of judgment, however, to change one's life-style radically. Self-generated change only adds to the level of the mourner's stress. Mourners suffer physical or emotional problems when, rather than slowing down the pace of their lives and simplifying their responsibilities during their grief, they increase both. Accelerating change increases both vulnerability and disorientation, and it decreases the ability to solve problems.[1] Medically speaking, the need to become very busy after the loss of a significant other occurs when the endocrine complex is high in the bloodstream, during the period of *searching* described in Chapter 6.

3. "This is a private matter."

A third common misunderstanding about mourning is that mourners ought to grieve privately. If one assumes that mourning should be short but continues to feel disoriented, and if one thinks it best to keep busy but no longer has the energy to do so, then one often assumes that something is wrong. To avoid alienation from others, then, many mourners decide to keep their mourning a private matter.

Almost all studies of mourners have revealed that mourners worry about whether it is necessary to hide their grief in order not to be thought of as crazy. This seems to be the notion of "out of sight, out of mind" applied to social relationships. Some mourners are so successful in masking their disorientation and sense of loss that even close relatives have been deceived. When asked how the mourner is handling the loss, relatives may answer, "Oh, really well," because they do not see the mourner crying.

Some authorities have called the attempt to hide the characteristics of mourning as the "religion of privatism." This happens when mourners believe their feelings to be so abnormal that if others really knew what was going on in their thoughts and emotions, they would be rejected and ostracized. The irony of this way of thinking is that persons who have to remain "private"—cut off from the very people they need—*do* become disoriented and crazy. Privatism fails to provide the basic cues of orientation needed for healthy living when major change occurs.

Frequently privatism is confused with the need for solitude. It is necessary to draw away from others from time to time in order to reflect on life, rethink priorities, and reorder activities. Solitude helps us reassess ourselves, in order to reenter social relationships. Privatism, however, is an attempt to shield one's sense of self by rejecting social relationships.

4. Mourning is for women only

A fourth misunderstanding is that men are not affected as much by loss as are women. Because many men do not show their grief, it is often assumed that they recover faster than women, that they do not need the support of others to overcome their grief, or that they are not as disoriented by major loss as women. Widespread research shows that each of these assumptions is false.[2]

Not only are men as vulnerable as women, but in some disease categories—such as congestive heart failure, myocardial infarction, and hypertension—widowed men are at higher risk level than women. As James J. Lynch put it, "Loneliness and grief often overwhelm bereaved individuals and the toll taken on the heart can be clearly seen. As the mortality statistics indicate, this is no myth or fairy tale—all available evidence suggests that people do indeed die of broken hearts, men as much as women."[3] The misperception that men are not as greatly affected seems to be based on societal expectations that men need to show their grief minimally in order to demonstrate their manliness.

5. "Forget it!"

Many mourners are advised to forget their loved ones, to set their losses behind them in order to get on with living. Yet many mourners report their greatest fear is that they will

forget. Some mourners conclude that since they cannot readily recall the details immediately preceding their loss, they
must be losing their minds or becoming senile. This advice
to forget is given not for the sake of the advised, but for the
comfort of the advisor. Such advice only disorients mourners
further. No researcher yet has documented that people ever
forget those they lose. What researchers do find, however, is
that the loss may be so painful that memories of loved ones
are repressed.

Because of these five misunderstandings, and others,
mourners may fail to tell their stories for fear that their experiences may be thought abnormal. They fear being ostracized by well-meaning but uninformed friends. It is important
that you tell your story as you experience it and keep telling
it as long as you feel that it needs to be told. Telling your
story is your way of understanding mourning.

2

Using the Concept of Disease to Tell Your Story

Is mourning an illness or a normal experience? That question is an issue among physicians and other health care professionals. In practice, most health care professionals treat mourning as an illness, even though medical and other health care research over the past decade finds the opposite to be true. Although pastors, educators, and others in the helping professions have traditionally understood mourning as normal in life when society was largely rural, they have tended to treat it as a disease since society became urban.

A look at medical, psychological, and theological insights will help clarify the question, What is mourning? How you and those you turn to for help answer the question will make a significant difference in how you tell your story following the loss of a loved one.

Evidence that mourning is a disease is persuasive when static methodologies of research are used. Researchers comparing the health of mourners with nonmourners find mourners vulnerable to both illness and premature death. As early as 1944, for example, Erich Lindemann found that mourners are at high risk levels for seven deadly diseases: myocardial infarct (the so-called heart attack), cancers of the gastrointestinal tract, hypertension (high blood pressure), neurodermatitis (chronic itching and eruptions of the skin, particularly in areas of heavy perspiration and in the webbing of the fingers and toes), rheumatoid arthritis, diabetes, and thyrotoxicosis (thyroid malfunction, most frequently seen in women).[1] Recent studies have confirmed Lindemann's early work.[2] In a study of cardiac patients, Dr. James Lynch found that mourners run two- to two-and-one-half times the normal risk for myocardial infarct when compared to nonmourners, and, depending on the region in which they live, three- to three-and-one-half times the risk for cancers of the gastrointestinal tract.[3] To the so-called "deadly seven" should be added chronic depression, alcoholism and other drug dependencies, malnutrition (both under and overnutrition), and electrolyte disorders in which the blood chemistry, particularly salts, are out of balance. Both objective and subjective studies indicate that mourners frequently are plagued by psychosomatic illnesses: headaches (particularly the migraine variety), low-back pain, frequent bouts with colds and flu, excessive fatigue, impotence, and significant sleep disturbances.[4]

Because of mourners' high vulnerability to illness, many physicians have responded by prescribing therapy in which characteristics of mourning are suppressed. In 1980, for example, it was found that 87% of physicians in Illinois assumed a "standard of care" that called for prescribing either a barbiturate or tranquilizer for mourners at the time of loss, and 83% of those physicians believed that should still be "standard of care" one week after the loss.[5] Less than 30% of them thought mourning would be a problem warranting prescriptions six months after the loss of a loved one. Given the common standards in medical education, we can assume that physicians in other parts of North America are not much different in their behavior from physicians in Illinois.

The medical profession is not alone in understanding mourning as disease, however. As many as 89% of the general public polled in 1980 understood mourning basically to be an illness, whose characteristics must be suppressed either by use of medicine or alcohol or through sheer determination or exercise of faith. Most of those polled thought it appropriate for physicians to prescribe drugs as a means for suppressing the symptoms. Many over-the-counter medications are purchased for the same purpose.

Medical research indicates that characteristics of grief are symptomatic of changes which have major physical, emotional, and spiritual consequences. Contrary to the popular opinion that mourning ought to be short or that the best way of handling mourning is to suppress its characteristics, medical research demonstrates that it is highly unlikely that any person can be unaffected in profound ways by the loss of a loved one.[6]

What the findings from medical research do not indicate, however, is that the majority of mourners are able to adapt to their loss in healthy ways. As so often is the case with medical inquiry, the focus is on contagion or dysfunction. As a consequence, there is a tendency to treat everybody experiencing the *dis*-ease of mourning in the same way. The best that can be determined is that between 5-15% of the population have unhealthy grief reactions. The overwhelming majority of mourners adapt healthily to their loss. As will be apparent later, the characteristics of mourning are usually signs of adaptation. Yet 85% of physicians and 89% of the general population believe it appropriate to suppress these characteristics of mourning. As a consequence, both physician and patient often fail to relate normal characteristics of mourning to behavior appropriate to preserve health.

The concept of disease is a helpful warning to get your story straight and to be honest about the symptoms of disorientation. Major loss is a threat to both your quality of life and longevity. However, to use the concept of disease as the primary guide for telling your story will force you into the roles of a patient.

Five Factors for Healthy Mourning

While research is still ongoing, five factors have been found useful in identifying those mourners who are likely to adapt healthily. Mourners most likely to adapt are persons who (1) maintain a nurturing, supportive social network, (2) have adequate nutritional balance daily, (3) have adequate fluid intake, (4) engage in daily range-of-motion exercise, and (5) maintain daily rituals of rest. The first three factors are the most important for both short- and long-range health assessment, and the last two are important for long-range health.

1. A Nurturing, Supportive Social Network

Of these factors, maintaining a nurturing, supportive social network is the most important. At a recent forum of the American Heart Association, researchers disclosed that loneliness increases the risk of illness and premature death. People cut off from society—without spouses, friends, or community ties—have a death rate twice as high as those of the same age who are socially involved. Drs. Lisa F. Berkman and Lester Breslow, in their ongoing study of 4,725 men and women between the ages of 30 and 69 in Alameda County, California, have found that being married, staying in frequent touch with friends and relatives, and belonging to a church or other social group are important factors for maintaining health after significant loss.[7]

Scientists have known for a long time that even the most intelligent and emotionally balanced person becomes disoriented when deprived of human contact over long periods of time.

Participation in mutual-help groups, telephone networks, and regular social activities like attendance at weekly worship seem crucial if a mourner is to maintain vitality. Everyone, it seems, needs a viable social network in order to keep their orientation.

2. Adequate Nutritional Balance

Having an adequate nutritional balance is the second most important factor. Without social interaction, the loss of appetite or the use of "junk" and "quickie" foods are more likely. High-risk health habits such as smoking, heavy consumption of alcohol, and erratic weight control are far more likely to be found among the socially isolated.

Many people are misinformed about nutrition and assume that only caloric intake is important. Weight loss or gain of 10 pounds from precrisis weight does not appear to be significant, but those mourners who gain or lose more than 25 pounds are most likely to have physiological and emotional problems. Among other things, there is growing confirmation that weight change within the latter range signals suppression of the immunological system.[8] Besides maintaining stable weight, however, mourners need daily portions of food from each of the four basic food groups:

- *Milk*—yogurt, cheese, ice cream, cottage cheese
- *Meat*—lean red meat, poultry, or fish
- *Fruit and vegetables*—as fresh and unprocessed as possible
- *Grains*—whole grains or fortified or enriched grain products

No matter how different people are in age, race, size, appearance, activity, or religion, each person needs the same nutrients: protein, fat, carbohydrates, vitamins, minerals, and water. Nutrition experts Carol West Suitor and Merrily Forbes Hunter summarize our nutrition needs:

- Each food group makes an important, distinctive nutritional contribution.
- Each food group lacks at least one essential nutrient.
- No one food or food group, taken alone, provides adequate amounts of all the essential nutrients.
- There is no one food which is essential to good nutrition.
- Use of a variety of foods from each group helps assure desirable intake of nutrients.[9]

3. Adequate Fluid Intake

Mourners have a tendency to override their sense of thirst. Adequate fluids, the amounts varying depending on gender and body weight, are necessary to carry away the body's toxic waste and to maintain appropriate electrolyte balance. Mourners need to drink more fluids than they feel they need. They frequently complain of tightness in the throat, diminished appetite, and "thick tongues." Alcohol or beverages with caffeine, which tend to cause further dehydration, should be avoided. Beverages with caffeine include coffee, colas, and many premixed beverages.

4. Daily Exercise

The fourth most important factor is daily full range-of-motion exercise. If muscles are to provide the appropriate pumping functions for nourishing and cleansing the body, they must be kept in good tone. For the person with sedentary habits, reasonable daily exercise is doubly important. Walking vigorously for more than 20 minutes at a time each day, various stretching regimens, and aerobic activities are examples of appropriate exercise. Regular exercise is also the most effective means for controlling depression. Those chemicals of the brain which cause feelings of alertness and happiness are stimulated in exercise. Transitory bodily discomfort, structural stress, and inadequate oxygenation of the blood are often relieved by exercise.

5. Daily Rest

Particularly for those who believe that mourning is best handled by the inappropriate assumptions of "out of sight/ out of mind" and "suppress problems by keeping busy," rest needs to come at the same time in each 24-hour cycle. Many people believe that if they cannot maintain their precrisis sleep routine or have the same level of sleep they had before their loss, they cannot rest. Instead, it is important that regular rituals for rest are followed even if it is impossible to sleep.

Many mourners make the mistake of continuing to work into the night because they are restless when they lie down. Then they begin to sleep later and later into the day. In a matter of a few weeks, their rest cycle is radically altered—sleeping in the daytime and staying up at night. Their internal clocks, what scientists call the circadian rhythms, are then unsynchronized with the rest of society and the usual areas of orientation which provide the sense of place, time, and well-being.[10] As a mourner, you should maintain the same rest patterns. If you are unable to sleep throughout the night, you may find it necessary to rest for an hour at midday.

When you tell your story as a mourner, assess yourself using these five factors essential for physical health and well-being.

3

Using the Concept
of Feelings to
Tell Your Story

Curiosity about human behavior has led many American psychologists to focus on *abnormal* behavior. *Abnormal* usually refers to a mourner's inability to function in socially acceptable ways or to maintain health. Certain circumstances of loss are severely disorienting: (1) unexpected or sudden death in unusual or socially stigmatized situations such as suicide, homicide, and drug overdoses; (2) traumatic and cataclysmic circumstances such as major fires, train and plane accidents, earthquakes, and other natural disasters; and (3) circumstances in which the body of the deceased is either unrecovered or so badly mutilated as to make positive identification impossible.

Research in psychology has shown that certain individuals are especially vulnerable: those with unresolved grief from childhood experiences, such as loss of parents or siblings; those with previous history of mental illness, particularly depression or schizophrenia; and those with multiple life crises, particularly near the time of the death of a loved one.[1]

Other circumstances recognized as abnormal are neurotic conflicts that were part of preexisting relationships (such as excessive dependency, hostility, and procrastination) and absent or delayed grieving—when grief is so painful that loss is either denied or repressed at all costs. Unfortunately, because mourning is widely misunderstood, individuals with these experiences may be viewed by the community as recovering well because they do not "break down" or "fall apart" emotionally.

As helpful as these findings are, emphasis on the abnormal has left many in the helping professions unable to differentiate between what is normal and what is abnormal in the mourning process. Diagnosing and labeling specific grief characteristics as abnormal, based on short-term interviews, has led to much misunderstanding and mismanagement of mourners.

Not all psychological research has focused on the abnormal, however. Particularly in Europe, considerable emphasis has been given to describing what is normal in growth and development. Such efforts led to an understanding of *adaptation*—the concept that human beings adjust to changing demands of the environment. Research now documents the fact that as people mature, there are common tasks that need to be accomplished at specific times. The tasks of a toddler are distinctly different from the tasks of a young adult, for example. These insights led not only to the realization that children have unique conflicts to work through before becoming adults, but also to the recognition that failure to complete childhood tasks before adulthood impedes adult functioning and may lead to an adult's inability to cope with life crises.

Four Tasks

Specific tasks relative to loss need to be accomplished at specific times in growing up and at times of major change in life. Harvard professor J. William Worden, who has spent much of his professional life studying life-threatening illness and life-threatening behavior, has identified four tasks for mourners:[2]

1. Accepting the Reality of Loss

The first task of mourning requires facing the reality that the loved one is dead. Very young children do not have the concept of irreversibility. In their experience, everything uncomfortable—hunger, soiled clothes, emotional upset—can be reversed. Their mother and father make it so. At some point in children's lives, however, the irreversible is encountered, even if their parents have been overly protective. Most mourners have had prior experience with the irreversible—that over which they have no control—but still they may imagine that they are in total control of their lives.

Even in adults imagination sometimes leads to unrealistic expectations. Only as imagination is confronted by realities are fantasies brought into control. I refer to this phenomenon as *perceptual confirmation*.[3] Despite what is imagined—good or bad—it is the ability to see, hear, touch, taste, or smell that orients human beings. The first attempt to confirm loss perceptually is when a mourner dares look at the remains of the deceased. Erica and Warren, for example, could not believe their son was dead. They had hugged him and bid him good-bye only 30 minutes before the accident. At the emergency room, however, when calling his name and touching his hands were not met by a response, the parents began the awful task of accepting the finality of his death.

2. Experiencing Grief

It is abnormal and even masochistic to seek pain, but it is also abnormal to deny pain consistently. We all tend to avoid pain, and many mourners try to run away from the pain of their loss. Some people even take flight to the extreme of avoiding all people and all places reminiscent of the one who died. No matter how far people attempt to flee or to what extent they may try to avoid pain, the disorientation of loss remains. Usually, because they are out of their familiar surroundings, their disorientation becomes more profound, and their problems multiply.

Rather than attempting to accelerate change in their lives, mourners should try to simplify and stabilize their lives. Linda and Gordon desired a baby so much that they wanted to initiate a new pregnancy as soon as possible. If they had done so, their problems would have been compounded by confusion of their feelings of grief for the lost child with their feelings of expectation for the wished-for child. Fortunately, for them and for their other children, they resolved the painful conflicts of their loss before starting a new pregnancy.

There is no way to avoid working through painful experiences. Some people seem to cope with the pain of loss better than others, just as some are able to bear greater physical pain than others. Unfortunately, however, human beings can no more run away from their problems than they can outrun their shadows.

3. Adjusting to an Environment in which the Deceased Is Missing

It is difficult to realize how important another person is until that person is gone. Absence of loved ones makes mourners painfully aware of the roles the deceased played in their lives and the cues they provided for orientation. When loved ones are no longer present, mourners are deprived of the sight, smell, sound, touch, and sometimes even taste which stimulated the senses and were part of their life orientation.

Much of the mourning process is the work of identifying how the individual now gone played important roles in life. Part of this work evokes feelings of anger, fear, and guilt. As a mourner you may find it appropriate to play out in your mind the things you failed to do for or with the deceased. Attempts to suppress these thoughts only leaves uncertainty and inexplicable anger.

Mrs. Angelo, a woman in her 40s, was no longer enjoyable to be around. She snapped at her friends; she nagged her family; she fought dark thoughts. One of her neighbors finally confronted her, inquiring about what could cause her personality to change from the pleasant person she had been. When the neighbor showed interest in her, Mrs. Angelo was able to identify the beginning of her persistent anger with the time a close friend died. In sharing her feelings and telling her story about how her life changed when the friend died, Mrs. Angelo confided that she had ignored her friend's need to talk the morning she was killed. "She was the one I always could talk to," Mrs. Angelo confessed, "but I couldn't listen to her." As she shared this pain with her neighbor, Mrs. Angelo not only found someone new in whom to confide, but she had begun to adjust to her changed environment.

4. Withdrawing Emotional Energy Focused on the Deceased and Reinvesting it in Other Relationships

I doubt that it is possible for mourners to complete the tasks of reorienting themselves without becoming interested in others. If mourners isolate themselves, they are likely to become severely disoriented and may die prematurely. If they invest their emotional energies only in themselves, they are likely to become chronically ill. Yet mourners have numerous problems to resolve if they are to invest their emotional energies in other relationships.

Unfortunately, society assumes that when a person has lost a spouse, the mourner no longer needs to touch and to be hugged. Psychologists have known for a long time that babies who remain untouched do not thrive. Society in general has incorporated this insight into many rituals that provide surrogate parenting. Similarly, counselors have known for a long time that adults who are untouched do not thrive, particularly those who are oriented to physical expressions of affection. Our society has not incorporated this insight into acceptable rituals of relating. People often are uncertain what behavior of touching by mourners is appropriate. For many mourners, this uncertainty leads to contradictory messages: "Be with other people, but not too close"; "Reach out for help, but do not be too emotional about it"; "Find companionship, but do not make any commitments."

To reinvest emotional energies in other relationships requires an environment in which people allow mourners to relate to others in ways that are orienting. It requires the permission of old friends to form new relationships. To make the adjustment may require learning how to handle mixed messages of family and friends. This task of reinvesting emotional energy in other relationships is encouraged by mutual-help groups described under *"Directory of Organizations"* at the back of this book.

Five Danger Signs

Some mourners need special help from professionals—both health care professionals and the clergy. Many characteristics of mourning that used to be thought of as abnormal are now seen as part of the adaptive process. There are at least five major warning signs, however, which—if they persist—indicate that grief has become pathological. If you are a mourner with any of these characteristics, seek help promptly.

1. Persistent Thoughts of Self-Destruction.

Most mourners report that from time to time they have wondered whether it is worth it to adapt or readjust to their loss. One widow said she felt so lonely at times that her mind kept focusing on how she could pursue death in order to be with her deceased husband. Later she concluded that she had other things to live for.

Fleeting ideas of self-destruction, both at the conscious and unconscious levels, are common. If as a mourner, however, you find yourself focusing consistently on self-destructive thoughts or making plans to destroy yourself, you should seek professional help.

2. Failure to Provide for Your Five Basic Survival Needs

Again, the five factors for maintaining a healthy, adaptive mourning process are: (1) maintaining a nurturing social network; (2) daily nutritional balance; (3) adequate fluid intake; (4) regular range-of-motion exercise; and (5) daily rituals for rest.

Inability to maintain any of these five factors on a daily basis is a warning signal that you may need help either from friends or from a member of a helping profession.

I suspect that every mourner fails to meet some of these needs some of the time, yet most still have the emotional and spiritual resources to correct the deficiencies before any dysfunction becomes irreversible. Just as it is extremely difficult to tell a humorous story in order to pull oneself out of an emotional funk, however, so it is often difficult to give proper attention to one's own needs. The encouragement of others is essential.

3. Persistent Mourning or Long-Term Depression

Grief does not always follow a regular pattern, but characteristics of mourning should change over the passage of time. If any one characteristic dominates for more than several months, this may be a warning signal. For example, a woman who had lost her son in a car accident still appeared chronically numb and in shock four months after his death. An elderly widower suffered from chronic depression into the second year after loss. These characteristics are symptomatic of the mourner's continuing dysfunction, and professional intervention is often necessary.

Another example of failure to adapt is the individual who has "no feelings" or does not express grief following loss. These individuals may be viewed by their families and friends as coping well because they do not "break down and fall apart." But they have not adapted to the basic change in their lives, and the longer they continue to leave this work unresolved, the more susceptible they are to major dysfunction later in their lives.

Nonadaptive behavior can occur when a change has been so traumatic and massive that there is no orienting context or network of support for the mourner. The collapse of a dam, war, a major fire, a hurricane or a tornado often causes such massive disorientation that individuals cannot begin a reorienting process without professional intervention.

4. Abuse of Controlling Substances Such as Alcohol or Drugs

Any time controlling substances are used on a regular basis, the user should promptly request professional assistance. It has been found that people who are referred to substance-abuse centers often have unresolved grief as the underlying cause of their problems. In some treatment centers, as many as 20% of the patients have failed to adapt to a major loss in their lives. Use of controlling substances should be understood as the attempt to suppress disagreeable symptoms. Unfortunately, suppression of disagreeable symptoms does not address the underlying cause of those symptoms.

5. Recurrence of Mental Illness

People who have been mentally ill or who have a blood relative who has been depressive or manic-depressive should be alert to recurrence of the illness. An assessment by a psychiatrist is important. Characteristics of mourning often mask mental illness. Any qualms about seeking help from a mental health specialist should be set aside. As with other illnesses, the earlier the diagnosis is made and treatment begun, the more likely prompt recovery will occur. If there is no family history of mental illness, it is unlikely to be a problem.

What should you do if any of these five warning signals are part of your life? If your major symptoms are physical, consult your primary physician. If your major symptoms are emotional, consult your therapist, counselor, or pastor. Ask whether they have experience in helping the bereaved or whether you should be referred to a specialist. Ask counselors to be explicit about what you should experience as they work with you. If the warning signals persist, it is important that you inform your counselors.

Using the concept of feeling to tell your story will alert you to what is abnormal. By being aware of how some mourners have failed to adapt their lives in healthy ways, you can avoid their pitfalls. Focusing on the abnormal, however, will not guide you to what is normal. Recent research by mental-health specialists provides part of the guidance needed for telling your story. Identifying and completing tasks that orient you to adaptation are necessary parts of your story. To pretend that a loved one is not really dead, to avoid the warning signs of pain, to resist creating a new context for living, and to keep emotional energies invested in the deceased take as much work as the tasks of adaptation, but, unlike adaptation, they will leave you frustrated and disoriented.

4

Using the Concept of Faith to Tell Your Story

Anthropologists studying religions have identified ways by which people adapt to major changes in their lives by using patterned behavior called rites of passage.[1] In most Christian traditions, for example, soon after babies are born they are baptized. When children reach the age of decision, they are confirmed. When couples make a commitment of faithfulness, a ritual of marriage is performed. When persons assume major responsibilities for the community, they are installed. When joining special groups, they are initiated. When a person dies, a funeral is organized.

Rites of passage are symbols of trial-and-error procedures earlier generations developed to reorient individuals and communities after major changes. Almost all such rites remind participants of stories of ancestors answering questions about who they are (person), where they are and why (place), and how to measure themselves (time or season of life) in the light of life's changes.

In societies that have changed slowly, rites of passage allow mourners to face loss at both conscious and unconscious levels. Rites for the dead allow those affected not only to mourn as individuals in a specific time and place, but also to place that death in the context of all human finitude in all ages. Because of the relative youth and pluralism of North American societies, people do not have ways to conceptualize death as those in traditional societies have done.[2]

In many ways, rites of passage used by our ancestors could not function in the New World because there were not the population, cultural resources, or institutional traditions to support them. Diaries and journals of early settlers reveal that the pioneers were frustrated because of their small and scattered numbers and the absence of trained clergy, educators, and physicians. Making the best of their situation, many pioneers developed a philosophy which gave highest value to not having cultural resources or institutions. "Rugged individualism" became a rationalized life-style.

Not only were there few cultural resources and institutions to support traditional rites of passage, there were not the large extended families to share in the telling of corporate stories.

Later generations saw the old rites of passage as interfering with ways of making a living in the New World. Long rituals of mourning interfered with assembly line manufacturing. They did not promote quick success. And most importantly, they were based on obedience to priests and teachers rather than to captains of industry. The ways of the Old World, it was said, were not the ways of the New.

By rejecting the old ways, mourners in the New World are far more likely to incorporate into their own personalities both the causes and consequences of the death of a loved one. Rather than understanding death as part of the human condition, mourners are left feeling responsible for their losses. Rather than having a faith for living in which "for everything there is a season, and a time for every matter under heaven" (Eccles. 3:1), individuals whose losses remain a private concern are left with the task of rethinking and reassessing all of the consequences within their own small worldview. Modern mourners, therefore, are liable to more self-aggression and self-accusation. They are more vulnerable to individual loss because of a lack of cultural tools.

Our lack of adequate cultural perceptions about personal crises have resulted in at least three ways of telling one's story that endanger the physical and emotional health of mourners: the faith that (1) death is the end, (2) death can be controlled by magic, and (3) death does not exist.

1. Death Is the End

Nothing reveals true faith more decisively than a reaction to the loss of a loved one. For some mourners, the loss is total. Life has stopped not only for the deceased, but for the mourner as well. The deceased had provided all the cues for the mourner's living. Without them, the mourner feels forever and totally disoriented.

Mr. Shamanski's story is an example. Like many of his acquaintances, he had learned a craft and had been employed in the same factory for 35 years. His work had required long and hard hours, but he made sufficient money to buy a house within walking distance of the factory, to raise four children, and to develop a sufficiently large pension that would allow him and his wife to continue living the life-style to which they had become accustomed.

Mr. Shamanski never developed close friendships. He knew many people; he loved only one. He worked 48 hours in an average week, and when he was at home he puttered in his garden or watched television. He relied on his wife to discipline and supervise the children, to run the house, and to maintain family and social relationships. His name was on the church roster, but he seldom went to church except on Christmas and Easter.

When his wife died, Mr. Shamanski wished he had too. Though he had never discussed it with her, he had always assumed that he would die first, and all of the family's legal affairs were arranged accordingly. Now he assumed that he could not take care of his basic survival needs and that God was trying to punish him for some unknown reason. ''It was never meant to be for her to go first," he protested. "Now I have nothing to live for!"

For Mr. Shamanski, and many like him, life was not what he expected. Because his wife had done so much for him and he was so overly dependent on her, he felt there was nothing to live for now that she was gone. Death, for him, was the end.

Death does mean *end*, but from the perspective of biblical faith the word *end* refers to purpose or fulfillment of design. To the degree individuals root themselves in the identity of their people, those individuals assess their personal stories on the basis of how well they have met the requirements of their people's destiny: Have they been faithful to their heritage? Have they learned to care for one another? Have they prepared the following generation to walk in the ways of their ancestors and to live by their values? When individuals interpret their lives within the history of their people, their personal loss of a spouse, child, parent, or friend is provided with a context of meaning beyond oneself.

When understood in the sense of the Latin word *finis*, the word *end* may refer to an individual's termination or cessation. From the perspective of biblical faith, a person may seek fulfillment in the eternal body of Christ and yet accept personal termination. For example, many find orientation in the biblical passage: "So when what is mortal has been clothed with what is immortal, and when what will die has been clothed with what cannot die, then the Scripture will come true: Death is destroyed; victory is complete!" (1 Cor. 15:54 TEV). Death, then, does not define a person's life even though he or she, as an individual, dies.

2. Death Controlled by Magic

Many people believe that the best way of handling the disorientation of loss is to suppress or repress the characteristics of mourning. Some people try to suppress the characteristics of mourning by medications or alcohol. Others try either to make their disorientation into an illness or deny that they have feelings of loss at all. Still others, using the concept of faith, try to change the facts of loss through ritual manipulation.

Gil Moreland and his wife were parents of a 14-month-old son. They were also members of a group that believed that prayer alone would cure anything from colds to cancer. To seek help anywhere but through prayer, they believed, was to show a lack of faith in God. Quoting from the Bible, the pastor of the Morelands' congregation proclaimed: "What things soever ye desire, when ye pray believe that ye receive them and ye shall have them" (Mark 11:24 KJV).

When the Morelands' son became seriously ill, they prayed as they had been taught. In a matter of days, however, the flulike symptoms changed to high fever. Though the Morelands did not know it at the time, their son had meningitis, a dangerous inflammation of the membranes that envelope the brain and spinal cord.

Despite the deafness, blindness, locked jaw muscles, and swollen neck that developed, the Morelands did not seek medical care for their son. Their pastor assured them that these signs were "the devil's lies," which were testing their faith. They brought the child to church to be prayed over, believing that anyone for whom prayer is offered is healed in the ways the prayers expect, even though appearances suggest the contrary.

The Morelands believed that the same power of prayer that heals the sick also raises the dead. So they did their best when they found their son dead in his bed. In the story of magic, people believe that certainty of cure must precede the claiming of the cure. But the claiming of the cure is essential for insuring that healing occurs. Therefore, once the Morelands had committed themselves to curing their son's illness through prayer, they needed to continue to assert the cure if it were to happen.

I wish the tragedy of the Morelands' story ended here, but it did not. Their pastor declared that the Moreland's inability to heal their son or to raise him from the dead proved their faithlessness, and they were condemned by the congregation.

Fortunately, the Morelands' story is exceptional, but the magical use of religion against the facts of illness, suffering, and mourning is not that unusual. Using the cliché, "It's God's will" to explain every occurrence, in both daily living and in loss is the attempt to change an uncomfortable story by rejecting or suppressing the facts of suffering. The result is to trivialize human experience, something never done in biblical faith.

In his study of biblical faith, theologian H. Richard Niebuhr noted that people may dispute endlessly about the will of God, but when they do, it seems always on the basis of faith other than faith in the God of the Bible. Faith, he noted, comes not as a possession that we can hold in our own power and use to manipulate others, but as a gift.[3] Spiritual healing is strongly upheld in biblical faith, but spiritual healing is not ethereal and otherworldly. It is what today is called wholistic healing. Healing is not that which individuals wield as power over others, but comes as grace and is manifested in many ways—even through modern medical and psychological techniques. Spiritual healing is what I call *orientation*. Life is not perfect, but it can be lived to the fullest.

3. Death Does Not Exist

A third inadequate faith by which to tell one's story of loss is the belief that death does not exist at all. "Life is unending; death is a mirage," some people plead. Some philosophies imply that those who learn to control their minds and draw into the life of the mind can escape the mortality of the body. By living only through the mind, it is believed, people can avoid dying and grief. Like other manifestations of religion, this story has been romanticized to the point in which "leaving this world" is encouraged as a way of escaping all of life's discomforts.

Dan Johnson did not know anything about religions or philosophies that held that death does not exist, but he did know that he disliked "shows of emotion," "things that make people unhappy," and funerals. His faith was that the consequences of loss do not exist. After moving to the West Coast, he severed most of his ties to relatives in the Midwest. He found "the good life." He quickly ascended the management ladder of a large corporation, made many acquaintances, and played hard.

When Dan's widowed mother became seriously ill, he had her moved to an extended-care facility in his city. "It's expensive," he explained, "but at least I know what's going on. I don't trust the relatives. All they are interested in is how to get mom's money." As time passed, Dan found less and less reason to visit her. He was surprised when he received the phone call that she had died. He did not go to the nursing facility. "I would prefer to remember her as she was when I was a boy," he explained. And because no one knew her in his city, he arranged for "removal and disposal" of her remains by phone. The body was cremated and the ashes were disposed of at sea. "Out of sight, out of mind," was Dan's way of handling his loss. He seemed to believe that the death of his mother was unreal and that his loss was insignificant.

Two years later Dan discovered that he was not a mind apart from a body. Not only did he become chronically depressed, he also became a cancer patient.

When mourners consider loss as the end of life, try to control their mourning by magic, or deny the reality of loss—all attempts to suppress or repress the characteristics of mourning—they place their trust in worldviews for which life is defined by the disaster of their individual loss. As a consequence, they are cut off from those means by which one can adapt to a new situation.

Religion—like medicine, psychology, or other disciplines by which human beings try to understand themselves—can be used either to orient or further disorient the mourner. When it orients mourners, faith provides the means by which mourners can grasp their personal situation in the context of the human condition.

The crisis of losing someone can be the most disorienting event of a person's life. A person may feel that the loss cannot be borne. From the perspective of biblical faith, however, no realization of loss or changes in life are so overwhelming that the mourner is left without orientation.

When our two-year-old daughter was watching *The Wizard of Oz* on television, she became deeply alarmed by the appearance of the Wicked Witch of the West. As she buried her head under her mother's arm she exclaimed, "Mommy, it's so awful how can you look?" Her mother responded: "It is awful, but I know the end of the story, and that lets me look."

Biblical faith does not shield us from the facts of life. Rather, we are prepared to face those facts—people do lose, they do suffer, and they must die—because individual changes are placed in the universal context of God's will. In the biblical tradition, God's will is revealed through a people's history and through the telling of that history. Their history is a story of destiny. In the telling of that story, adherents of biblical faith find the outline and the purpose of their personal stories. For Christians, God's self-revelation in Jesus Christ is a revelation that the occasions of a person's suffering need not define that person's life. Because God does not disappear in the presence of imperfection—death, loss, or suffering—and is not manipulated by the magic of words or deeds, the human sufferer can live the seeming contradiction of growing though losing.

Just as good health habits help persons fight disease and coping skills prepare them to resolve the problems of change in appropriate ways, so prayer and meditation help individuals grow as human beings despite the disorientation of loss. As one father said (following the death by automobile accident of his young son), "It's as if all my life of Bible study, worship, and prayer has been preparation for living beyond this most painful moment." People may consciously work to overcome disorientation at times of loss when they place their individual stories in the larger story of life—a story hopefully learned well before the onset of a major crisis.

Through participation in the rites of passage—rituals in which universal values and models for thought and action are revealed—individuals discover both their own limits and a sense of order that transcends the present generation and the particular crisis.

Whether mourners have anticipated their loss or have been confronted without warning, their initial reaction is shock. Disbelief, uncertainty, and unfamiliarity require each mourner to ask the question, "What should I do?" At that point, the rite of passage called the funeral begins. Every religion and most communities have prescribed ways for returning to wholeness, of becoming reoriented. The older the tradition, the more rites of passage function unconsciously for answering questions about "What should I do?" and the less likely mourners are to understand how the rituals began or why they are helpful. Even to mourners who have not been active in a religion, the informal and formal rituals of the funeral allow them an appropriate way of saying good-bye to the deceased and of searching for reentry into normal life.

I have attempted to show both effective and ineffective, reorienting and disorienting, ways mourners tell their stories. Whatever your story, you cannot avoid including how you have been affected physically by your loss. From the medical perspective, you may not have perfect health, but you may find those guides by which to keep your physical health at the highest possible level.

Whatever your story, you cannot avoid including how your loss has brought you emotional pain and suffering. From the psychological perspective, you may find those guides by which to adapt to the new facts of life.

Whatever your story, you cannot avoid including how your loss has challenged your faith. From the theological perspective, you may find the guides by which to reorder your sense of trust. What follows in the next four chapters is a description of how many mourners described the impact of their loss and how they found their way to a story of new life.

5

When Mourning
Is Shock
and Numbness

Confusion and ignorance about mourning has led to a great deal of misunderstanding about what characterizes the emotions of loss. In this and the following three chapters, I will list the characteristics which tend to dominate adult mourners' lives as they try to adapt. The data is based on a study of 1200 adult mourners, each of whom I followed over a two-year period in order to record common experiences. The characteristics most dominant are correlated to the amount of time that has passed since the death of their loved ones.

I have included a graph summarizing the statistical data in each chapter. The scale on the left-hand side of each graph or figure (low = 1, high = 7) measures the intensity of the characteristics, based on the mourners' subjective assessment. Mourners were asked to make the assessment in comparison to the intensity with which they had experienced the characteristics previously in their lives.

The horizontal scale runs from two weeks to 24 months. The broken line mark (//) indicates that the scale is not uniform.

Intensity of the characteristics of mourning in the first two weeks after the death of a loved one

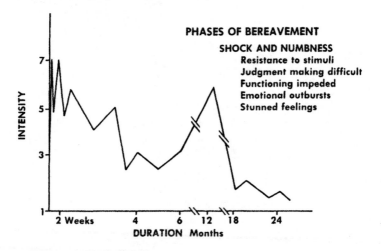

Characteristics of Mourning which Tend to Dominate in the First Two Weeks

Everyone has ways of handling major changes in life. For some, the death of a relative or friend is met with total disbelief, particularly when death was unexpected. For others, death brings relief, particularly when it has been preceded by suffering. Some people require a long time to organize the actions they will take to respond to their loss. Others promptly begin to organize themselves, making either a mental or written list of action steps. Still others wait for someone else to take over. While everyone has personal ways of coping, behind the differences tends to be a common set of characteristics. It is important to remember, however, that there are always exceptions to these characteristics.

Feeling stunned is the most common characteristic reported by mourners when loss occurs. It reveals the inability to separate what one feels from how one thinks. Many mourners, for example, report having asked their physicians or other staff personnel questions about the death of their loved ones, yet cannot remember the answer given. But these same individuals can clearly remember, even years later, how the people around them made them feel.

When change is unexpected, it is natural to become anxious and *resistant to stimuli*, as though one wished to make time stand still. The more others ask questions and the noisier or brighter the surroundings, the more difficult it is for mourners to cope. When in shock, people need others to remove them to a more sheltered area where stimuli can be diminished until they are over their initial disorientation. In the better-managed hospitals, for example, family rooms are available where colors are subdued, lighting low, and the noise level minimal. There staff know how to offer comfort with as little intrusion as possible until mourners begin to recover their wits, rather than to bombard them with questions to be answered and forms to be signed.

As their stunned feelings pass, mourners need to express *conflicting and competing emotions:* the need to cry, to be angry, to laugh and joke without fear of being ostracized. Reactions to loss may be marked by rapid swings of emotion. This may be frightening both to the mourners and to those around them, but the wide swing of emotion is appropriate and part of the process of recovering emotional equilibrium and orientation. We should be much more concerned with the person who is unable to express emotions of disorientation.

Until mourners are able to identify *what* they feel, they are unable to determine *how* they should act. John Garrison had that problem when his wife died unexpectedly. He had rushed her to the emergency room of their local hospital, expecting that physicians there would be able to revive her. When they were unable to do so, Mr. Garrison was stunned and unable to grasp the reality of his loss. Rather than expressing his sorrow as anger or as sadness, he had a flat affect—eyes glazed and face expressionless—but he did everything he was directed to do by the emergency-room staff. What he could not do, however, was make basic decisions or answer questions appropriately. Only when his son and daughter-in-law arrived and made the necessary decisions were the staff able to leave him unattended. Mr. Garrison was easy to work with because he was compliant, but the staff knew that until he got in touch with his own feelings, he would not begin to take charge of his own life.

In sharp contrast was Robert Hills, who, when his wife died while being examined in the emergency room, cried copiously and expressed anger at the staff for being unable to revive her and at his wife for having left him. But after his expressions of strong emotion, Mr. Hills was clear about what he needed to get done.

Expressing a wide spectrum of emotion is healthier than trying to express no emotion. Mourners may fear that if they give vent to the depth of their sorrow, they will be unable to bring themselves under control. They fear becoming hysterical. On the contrary, as soon as the high level of adrenalin has been metabolized from the system, they calm down. I have found that if a mourner is not reshocked or disturbed by inappropriate intervention of hospital staff or well-meaning friends and relatives, emotions are not "out of control" for more than 15 or 20 minutes.

As the emotions of shock and numbness pass and the adrenalin is metabolized in the blood stream, most mourners feel a deep fatigue. It is appropriate to pause to give the body a chance to return to a more normal energy level. Beverages like coffee, tea, or soft drinks with caffeine, plus some quickly digestible bread, cracker, or cookie will help mourners recover energy quickly and provide a sense of comfort.

Functioning is impeded when people experience shock. If the shock occurs in a health care institution, individuals should be placed in the family room until such time as they feel recovered. People need to be able to process stimuli effectively. When they reach the point where they can ask questions and remember the answers, and when they can begin to make plans, they are recovering from shock and are ready to function. For most, it takes between 20 and 30 minutes to recover sufficiently so as to drive a car safely. It is important to recognize that reaction time to stimuli—the coordination of fine muscles with thought processes and the ability to recognize situations that may endanger lives—is compromised when people are emotionally shocked.

Making judgments is difficult, not because mourners are unable to make individual decisions (such as which funeral director to call, whether an autopsy is appropriate, or what they should do next), but because there has been a radical change in mourners' ability to concentrate. They find it difficult to follow the implications of one decision through the usual series of consequences. Until such time as mourners are fully responsive again, it is unethical to ask them to sign "informed consent" forms or to make any irreversible decisions. When anyone is rushed or pushed by well-meaning people to make decisions too difficult at the time, those people should be told to wait. Seldom does any decision need to be made before mental faculties are once again ready to function, except when someone's life is at stake. The anxieties of well-meaning relatives and friends or the impatience of hospital staff are insufficient causes for pushing someone into making decisions.

The characteristics of shock and numbness seem to be most intense in the first two weeks—that period of mourning most people consider appropriate for grieving. These first characteristics of mourning are commonly recognized and understood. Unfortunately, however, they represent only the beginning of the mourning process—unfortunate because mourners will need to learn and to signal others that they have not yet returned to preloss functioning.

Telling Your Story

One of the first tasks for a new mourner is to decide who needs to know about the death. Many people make the decision to tell as few people as possible. "I don't see that my problems are anyone else's business," Elizabeth Collins, a middle-aged woman, said rather matter-of-factly about her mother's death. She had returned to her home town from a large metropolitan city to bury her mother's remains. All she wanted, she instructed the funeral director, was a simple service for a few relatives. The usual obituary in the county newspaper would not be printed in time to inform people either of her mother's death or funeral.

Mrs. Collins did not consider the fact that her mother had been part of the community all of her life, and while not an active leader, had related to people in quiet ways in her church, a card club, and a senior citizens hobby center. Word of her mother's death spread through the community quickly. More than 100 people came to the funeral, and only half that number could be accommodated in the funeral chapel. Had others who loved her mother and who also needed ways to reorient themselves to her loss been allowed appropriate channels for expressing their grief, the daughter would not have been caught off guard. Mrs. Collins thought she knew what all her problems were. She sought to control them by rejecting the possibilities that her mother's death created problems for others too.

The decision to exclude, rather than include, others in the funeral may lead to many problems later. When those who had expected to be informed become angry at the next of kin instead of expressing sorrow over their sense of loss, they become further disoriented. Survivors sometimes forget that their loss is also a loss for others.

A second task for telling your story is to discover how to involve others who "need to do something." In more traditional communities there are established rituals that help channel mourners' needs to help. Rituals such as preparing meals for the immediate family, decorating the church or funeral chapel, answering the telephone in order to relieve family from interruptions, and providing transportation for guests coming from out of town are examples of activities which can be organized.

It is important for you to let others assist you in the funeral—for their sakes and yours. If you are like many new mourners, you will discover that one of the most important gifts you receive is the presence of others as fellow mourners. When mourners are together, individuals have permission to grieve openly and honestly. Your own story is only part of the larger story that needs telling.

After experiencing a loss, mourners often feel they should be doing something, but may not know what can be done. A third task is to channel these feelings into plans for the funeral. Questions such as "Whom shall you tell?" "How should you act?" "What should you do, when?" are answered in the rituals of leave-taking when others are permitted to be part of the funeral. You may have some ideas about how you would like the funeral to be arranged. Discuss these ideas with your family, pastor, and funeral director. If you do not know what you want, ask them to suggest options for your consideration. Review assignments of family and friends in order to anticipate problems early enough to resolve them. Part of your responsibility is exploring possible options.

A fourth task is to take time to be reflective. Use of devotional literature and prayers helps many mourners find adequate words by which to identify and express their feelings and to better understand their disorientation. Ask your pastor or a friend to provide times in which you and those around you can meditate and reassess what is happening to you.

Another task, one which will take some mourners a long time to complete, will be to get the facts of their loss. Often mourners try to tell their story without the facts. They avoid returning to the police, physician, nurse, or onlookers who were present at the time of their loved one's death. Nevertheless, these same individuals spend a great deal of energy acting out the scenario of their suspicions. Sometimes these suspicions become so negative that mourners become paranoid—overwhelmed with feelings that other people are trying to take advantage of them or destroy them.

It is very common and normal to go over and over the story of your loss. It is important to find those people who will allow you to continue to review your story as you attempt to get the facts. Often this process is so slow that both you and those who would like to support you assume that no progress is being made in putting your story together. Those mourners who have written down their innermost thoughts or kept a diary have found that the stories do change, subtly and slowly perhaps, but decisively. As facts are uncovered, mourners are able to make sense out of what occurred.

Part of the task of getting the facts is to picture where the loss took place. This action becomes particularly important in situations in which death was unexpected. Erica and Warren, for example, could not get control over their nightmares about their son's motorcycle accident until they were able to find the deputy sheriff who had covered the case and had him escort them to the site of the accident. There, with his help, they were able to recreate the tragedy in their minds. As is so often the case, the reality of the setting was less traumatic than what they had imagined. Being able to see where the accident occurred helped Erica and Warren bring their suspicions under control.

In the hospital in which I have my office, a memorial service is offered monthly in order to give survivors an opportunity to come back to the site of their loss. By returning to the hospital, the friends and families are able to articulate their questions and bring their loss into a more realistic perspective.

Getting the facts may also necessitate returning to the place where the remains of your loved one are buried. Observers may worry that mourners go to cemeteries too often. The paradox, however, is that the more mourners are thwarted from going, the more they feel obsessed to do so. On the contrary, the more mourners feel free to go to the site of the burial, the more they feel released from the obsession to go.

When mourning is shock and numbness, you will need the help of others to get your story into accurate form. Being able to know the facts, to visualize the setting, and to confirm your loss are all needed at a time when your own perceptions of reality are most distorted.

6

When Mourning
Is Searching
and Yearning

Characteristics of Grief which Tend to Dominate in the First Four Months

For mourners, shock and numbness begin to give way rather quickly to a new set of characteristics. Mourners become *acutely aware of stimuli* in their yearning for the presence of their loved one, particularly as they search for familiar sounds, smells, and sights associated with the deceased. They become sensitive to stimuli as they feel capable of coping with the consequences of change. Mourners should not attempt to make decisions, operate automobiles or other equipment, or commit themselves to any course of action until such time as they are able to respond appropriately to sight, sound, smell, taste, and touch.

A second characteristic is a shift from the mood swings described in the previous chapter to *anger directed at other people* and to *guilt focused on oneself*. Viola Canni, for example, verbally attacked the physician as soon as he came into the room after her husband died. Rather than acting defensively or trying to ignore her anger, the physician encouraged her to be explicit about what made her angry. This encouraged her to process her feelings, and she discovered that contrary to appearances, she was not angry at her husband's physician at all, but rather at her husband, whom she feared had left her in financial jeopardy. Even though her anger was misdirected, Mrs. Canni's feelings of anger were appropriate insofar as anger warns others when someone feels that their integrity and ego are in danger of being violated. Contrary to popular opinion, one cannot prevent anger once it has been stimulated. The only option is whether to express it appropriately or destructively.

Guilt is often anger turned on oneself. All the mourners in the case studies of Chapter 1 felt considerable guilt surrounding their loss. When Linda and Gordon lost their baby, they worried about what they had or had not done during Linda's pregnancy: Had she eaten something that harmed the fetus? Had her amniotic fluid become contaminated in some way? Had she not gotten enough rest? Had Gordon been supportive enough of her? Some of their friends reinforced feelings of guilt by suggesting that their loss was "God's way of telling you that you are not close enough to him."

In the early part of this century, psychiatrists were critical of the emphasis of religious leaders on guilt. As with the comment from Linda and Gordon's friends, guilt was often used as a manipulative device to make the vulnerable think or behave in a certain way. As a result, many people came to the conclusion that guilt is an inappropriate emotion. This perception led psychiatrist Karl Menninger to ask: "Whatever became of sin?" [1]

Wrongs committed cannot be addressed unless it is possible to identify what they are. Feelings of guilt not only warn an individual when senses of propriety are being violated by unusual behavior, but they also warn when someone is being extended beyond their ability to cope. Persons who feel they have lost control over a situation often feel guilty.

Whether they lose a baby, a 19-year-old son, or a spouse, mourners feel guilty. As part of that process of sorting out their responsibility, guilt alerts them to the fact that "something is wrong." Rather than trying to suppress the feelings, mourners should express them in order to be able to discern what the limits of their responsibility are for events over which they have no control. Only in clarifying what they should feel guilty about—either through omission or commission—can they know what they need feel no guilt over. An example of this process comes from the Old Testament character Job, who expected to be spared loss of family, health and wealth, and therefore wrestled with all manner of possibilities as to why bad things were happening to him.

Intensity of the characteristics of mourning in the first four months after the death of a loved one

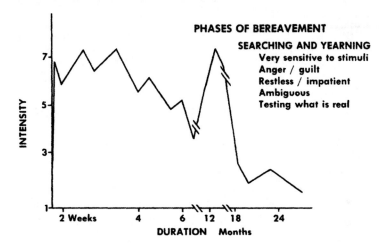

Another frequent characteristic of mourners is *restlessness and impatience*. When mourners describe this feeling as "nervousness" or "my nerves," they are speaking about the inability to relax. This happens particularly in the large muscles of the arms and legs, and then radiates out as "nervousness" or twitches to the rest of the body. This condition is caused in part by a high level of adrenalin in the blood which irritates the nerve endings of the large muscles. The major muscles are designed to contract easily and do so with the slightest stimulation. It is possible for them to relax, however, only when the adrenalin levels in the blood are lowered. Mourners' feelings of anxiety, their need to "do something," and agitation are manifestations of body chemistry.

This condition also seems to be one of the foundations for high motivation. Because motivation will diminish later, mourners should find those activities that help most in discovering new roles for relating socially. If the mourner is not part of a nurturing social network, restlessness may indicate the need to find a bereavement support group or other social outlet in which orientation can be provided. Involving oneself while motivation is high will help to establish the support system so necessary when motivation is low.

Another characteristic of this time of mourning is ambiguity. While mourners are searching and pining for their lost ones, they often find it difficult to make judgments. Because mourners are obsessed with the feelings of change that follow a loss, they find it difficult to concentrate on a single train of thought and to follow it through to its implications and consequences. One man complained that his mind was like a "grasshopper's, jumping all over the place." Marge knew that she had to make some decisions about her husband's estate. She sought the counsel of an attorney and collected all of the required documents. Unfortunately, the options set before her by her counselor required more concentration than she seemed capable of mustering. As a result she kept changing her mind.

The intellectual task at this time seems to be the testing of what is real. Mourners often ask, "Why me?" "What does it mean for me?" "Who was responsible for this change?" It is not enough for individuals to have a philosophical and theological framework in which to interpret these basic changes of life. To adapt, mourners need to reexamine and reassess their priorities. Searching and yearning are most acute among mourners who have suffered unexpected change or loss. Even those who anticipated the death of their loved ones, however, are still sensitive to the loss of orienting cues associated with a loved one.

Searching and yearning seem to be highest between two weeks and four months after the loss, peaking again around important dates in the life of the mourner, like anniversaries and holidays. In this period of uncertainty about what is real, it is important that mourners respect the process by which they sort through what are appropriate and inappropriate expectations for themselves. It is important for them to delay decisions as much as possible, particularly those that cannot be reversed.

When You Are Uncertain about How Your Story Should Go

Most mourners report that during this period when searching and yearning are high, their motivation "to do something" is also high. Some mourners go on traveling or buying binges. Others seek to make basic changes in their lives: changing their jobs, moving from houses in which they have lived—even changing spouses and friends. For example, the incidence of separation or divorce among couples who have lost a child at birth or shortly thereafter is exceptionally high in the two years following their loss.

Although it is easy to understand this flight from the problems their loss has created, such a reaction is just the opposite of what is needed for healthy living. While the characteristics of searching and yearning are high, physiologists know that the endocrine complex, which irritates nerve endings, is high in the bloodstream. Further accelerating change keeps that endocrine complex high and creates more "nervousness." Many mourners fail to slow down and give themselves a chance to regenerate. Our ancesters, in their rituals of grief, showed the wisdom of slowing down, having fewer responsibilities, and accepting limitations on what they expected for themselves.

Unfortunately, in today's urban and technological society, those around mourners who want to spare them as much suffering as possible are usually overly eager to encourage changes that give the impression that the mourners have finished grieving. The social support that is so basic to human orientation then causes further disorientation.

When Your Story Becomes Bizarre

Many people become fearful about themselves when they experience the bizarre. Linda and Gordon, the couple who lost their baby at birth, feared that Linda was "losing her mind" when several months later she found herself unable to throw out a rotting cucumber. Linda was a gourmet cook and regularly weighed her cooking ingredients. One day while preparing an Italian dish, she placed the cucumber on the kitchen scales. In an instant, she became aware that the cucumber was the exact weight of the baby she had not been permitted to see. She took the cucumber in her arms, cradled it and cried. She could not throw it out, because she was identifying it with her lost baby—at least in one aspect. Other couples report similar bizarre experiences, such as being awakened early in the morning by the crying of their dead baby. This is called *phantom crying*, and is similar to phantom pregnancy. Both are startling experiences based on realities of the past, but which do not fit with what is known to be real in the present.

Erica and Warren, the parents who lost their son in a motorcycle accident, found that they could not rearrange, discard, or give away any of their son's possessions. Erica found herself clinging to scraps of doll clothing that her son had used as a small child. Warren secretly treasured a lock of his son's hair. At the conscious level both parents knew that it was important to change. Their other children needed the space and could use their brother's possessions. Nevertheless, by clinging to objects that they identified with their deceased son, Erica and Warren were able to express their grief in ways that they were not able to articulate. They worried, however, that in clinging to objects associated with their son they would be ostracized by their friends and that this behavior was abnormal.

Marge, the widow who lost her husband after a long illness, referred herself for counseling because she feared that she was going "crazy." When asked to describe the occurrences of the "craziness," she mentioned an event that happened when she was working in her kitchen one afternoon. Around 5:45 she moved into the living room and sat down in a chair. She heard noises that she thought sounded like steps on the porch, and then she heard noises that sounded like a key in the lock. She reported that "immediately the hair on the back of my head stood on end. I just knew that my husband had come back."

Marge soon realized that what she was doing was repeating a pattern she had established early in her marriage. She would prepare dinner and then clean up and wait for her husband to come from work. While she was sitting in the chair in the living room that afternoon, she was thinking about her husband, how much she missed him, and about how, if he were alive, he would be coming home about that time. She undoubtedly did hear noises, but, as is typical when individuals are disoriented by rapid changes, Marge misread the stimuli, making them mean what she was already thinking. Other widows and widowers speak of how their deceased spouses return from the dead. Some research indicates that a majority of mourners have this kind of experience. In every case I have investigated, there has been a stimulus or cue that had been part of the mourner's life prior to the loss. The smell of cologne or bath oil used by the deceased or familiar sounds or sights trigger memories of the one lost.

When mourning was understood as an illness, it was easy to jump to the conclusion that bizarre episodes were delusional and probably symptomatic of psychosis. Understanding mourning as a normal process of adaptation, however, allows for understanding these bizarre episodes as part of the adaptive process.

Why do they happen? Let me illustrate from my own life. The evening before I was to leave on a lecture tour, it was my turn to put our 18-month-old daughter to bed. I had given her a bath. I had put her in her nightclothes; I had read her a story; we had said our prayers. By that point it was time for her to be asleep. Instead of going to sleep, however, she began to bark like a dog. My first reaction was to think she was misbehaving, but then I heard the neighborhood dogs barking. Like every other alert infant, she was mimicking the stimuli around her. Like every other mature and responsible adult, I had learned long ago to filter out such extraneous stimuli—except when I am in crisis. Then, like every human being, I open myself to a far wider spectrum of stimuli in an attempt to discover cues by which to become reoriented.

Psychologists have long been able to document how an individual in isolation can remain oriented to person, place, and time only by memory. People learn to make sense out of their lives very early by relating to specific people, feeling comfortable in familiar environments, internalizing a sense of time and season. The major work of growth and development for infants is to make these cues into habits of thought and action. Familiar individuals, comfortable places, and the framework of days and seasons become so much a part of life that their influence is not questioned. They become such familiar cues that they become a part of the unconscious. Just because a loved one is gone does not mean that the influence of the deceased stops. Even under normal circumstances, adults can still hear the voices of absent parents telling them to get up or perform a task.

What should you do about these bizarre experiences? Let them happen. You do not need to be able to analyze such experiences in order for them to function as part of your efforts to be reoriented. It is helpful to many people to know that these experiences are usual and common. For some people it is important to understand them. Like dreams, bizarre episodes are fragments of life momentarily displaced. While bizarre episodes may take many forms, for most people they do not occur after the fourth month. My research hypothesis is that the bizarre—mental and emotional episodes experienced out of the usual contexts of person, place, and time—reflect body chemistry under stress. The extra sensitivity to stimuli, particularly those which were orienting cues associated with a loved one, can cause mourners to overread or misinterpret reality. Bizarre episodes may be part of your story.

7

When Mourning Is Disorganization and Depression

When mourners shift from testing what is real to being aware of the consequences of loss, they feel emotionally disorganized. The extent of this disorganization depends on the amount of energy and mental concentration required to accomplish basic tasks. Mourners most often compare their functioning against the functioning of others as part of the reorienting process—testing themselves against what is seen as reality in others.

A more important comparison is the one of preloss functioning with postloss functioning. People do not function as well when they are mourning as when they are not mourning, and they should not expect to.

Warren, an insurance executive, took great pride in the fact that he could keep documents from piling up on his desk. Following the loss of his son, however, he seemed unable to process the paper with the same efficiency. Caroline Noble, a homemaker, found that it was all she could do to prepare the meals for her family, get the children off to school, and do the laundry. This was in marked contrast to the highly organized and efficient way she ran her home prior to the death of her husband. Before her loss she had considerable time for volunteer work and social activities, but now Mrs. Noble found herself with "no time."

The Characteristics of Mourning from the Fifth Through the Ninth Months

Intensity of the characteristics of mourning between the fifth and ninth months after the death of a loved one

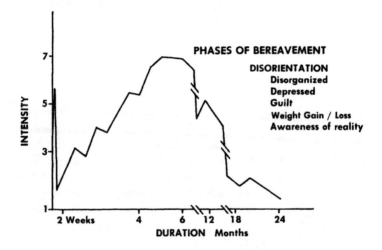

Many mourners find themselves angry from time to time, but more frequently they are depressed. *Depression* is one of the major emotions in the mourning process. Because onlookers often do not understand that this is normal, they may reprove the mourner's feelings. Yet it is during this time that mourners most need the support of people around them.

Being depressed interferes with the sense of work and personal worth. Most of the time people feel depressed for appropriate reasons. While persistent mourning can be the occasion for renewed bouts with mental illness, and the characteristics of mourning can mask the symptoms of clinical depression,[1] if there has been no personal or family history of mental illness, the chances of clinical depression are very small.

Many mourners report that they feel *physically enervated*, even after a night of rest. As a consequence, they do not feel motivated enough to tend to the five factors for good health—maintaining social contacts, balanced nutrition, adequate fluids, daily range-of-motion exercise, and regular rituals of rest. *Fluctuation of weight*—either through loss of appetite or compulsive eating—dry mouth and feelings of throat constriction, nervousness, and listlessness are common. Many mourners report problems with fine motor skills, and others report difficulty with recent recall and begin to fear that they are losing their minds. Because mental concentration is difficult, judgments are often inconsistent and difficult to make. Reality and roles remain confused. Nearly all individuals report that this period of bereavement is the most painful time of mourning.

Thomas Holmes and his colleagues have found through use of their "social readjustment scale" that out of 43 life events, loss of a loved one is the most stressful.[2] Holmes' findings have been confirmed by others.[3]

The period in which characteristics of disorganization seem most burdensome is between the fifth and ninth months. A significant number of mourners turn to the "sick role" in order to convince others that their feelings are legitimate. Mourners will come to physicians as patients with symptoms of reoccuring colds or flu—even more serious illness—as a way of getting medical attention.[4] While it is important to consult a physician when there is a concern about abnormal symptoms, it is also important to maintain healthy living habits.

Rather than turning to the sick role, mourners can benefit from this period of suffering by reexamining personal values and philosophies of living. During this period the theological task becomes both difficult and particularly important. Much of the mourner's emotional energy will be expended on reassessing life and establishing new priorities.

A physical exam between the fourth and fifth months is appropriate. If a mourner is developing an illness, the symptoms will usually appear during this time and yet be in an early enough phase of development to allow effective medical intervention.

Further, it may be important if one is chronically without energy to consult a physician about help with sleep. Use of mild doses of tranquilizers or antidepressants for a maximum of four out of seven nights is usually effective. After several weeks, most people become aware that they are getting up feeling more rested than when they go to sleep. It is important to remember, however, that part of the work of adaptation requires a period of depression and personal reassessment. Use of medications should be brief and under regular supervision of a physician. Altering eating habits may be as effective, and less costly, in helping induce sleep. About 90 minutes before bedtime a small amount of foods high in carbohydrates should be consumed. Research has found that as the carbohydrates are digested the brain releases a natural barbituate. It is good to prepare for rest while food is being digested. At bedtime avoid activities such as telephoning, housework, or business affairs that might be frustrating.

Upon arising, one should eat a good breakfast high in protein. As proteins are digested, the brain releases a natural amphetamine.

When usual ways of coping are disrupted, it is easy to fall into negative roles. Mourners are in danger of adopting one of three negative roles: (1) the derelict role, (2) the sick role, or (3) the despairing role.

1. Avoiding the Derelict Role

When a mourner is feeling disorganized, the motivation necessary for handling basic survival needs is often lacking. Reliance on friends becomes essential. Charles Thompson felt an acute need for social contact. He had lost his wife several years earlier, and he now found himself isolated and lonely.

Paradoxically, his behavior kept others away. Mr. Thompson appeared unkempt—often going days without shaving. He had not had a bath in months. In both appearance and smell he was offensive. What he wanted most was to have people with him when he ate. Without company he ate erratically. Sometimes he would start his day with breakfast, but other days he would go several hours before eating anything. He suppressed the feelings of loneliness and hunger by smoking heavily.

To compensate for lack of companionship, Mr. Thompson watched everything on television, including the late late movie, so that he would not have to lie awake and think about his plight. As a consequence he started getting up later and later in the morning, and within months he had succeeded in completely reorienting himself to sleeping through the day and being up at night—further cutting himself off from human contact. Finally he started taking over-the-counter medications to try to induce sleep, and he began drinking. By the time Mr. Thompson's family brought him to the clinic, he was badly malnourished (even though obese), drug dependent, and disoriented as to time and place.

2. Avoiding the Sick Role

When people are ill, they expect to be relieved from usual responsibilities, to be the center of care, and to take on a more passive role. If properly cared for, people who are ill become the center of others' attention. Rachel Quigley lost her baby at birth. She was in anguish over the loss of her wished-for child and found that others around her were very uncomfortable. Mrs. Quigley tried to talk with her husband about her feelings, but he rebuffed her efforts in an attempt to protect his own feelings. When she returned home, her husband and mother-in-law had put away all of the nursery furniture and baby clothes. When she found herself crying spontaneously at family gatherings, her brothers and sisters either got up and left the room or ordered her to get hold of herself.

About six months after the loss of her baby, Mrs. Quigley was feeling so bad that she went to her physician to see what was wrong. She had developed migraine headaches and had lost about 15 pounds. She found it difficult to eat even when she had an appetite.

Mr. Quigley and the family became concerned that she was ill. Family members talked with her about how she was feeling, brought in meals, called regularly, and expressed concern about her. She discovered that she would receive more of her family's attention if she were ill. Unfortunately, she also discovered that the more she wanted to feel good emotionally, the more ill she had to become. Only after professional intervention helped her identify the new role that she was taking with her family was Mrs. Quigley able to be explicit about how they could be more supportive of her needs. Often people near mourners do not know what to do and therefore behave in ways that ignore the mourner's disorientation. Turning to the sick role may be effective for a mourner to gain attention, but it does not lead to healthy adaptation.

3. Avoiding the Despairing Role

One of the tasks for mourners is to come to the realization that time cannot be turned back. The change that has occurred with the death of the loved one is irreversible. The paradox is that the more people want things to stay the same—and behave accordingly, the more things become different and often ugly as mourners fail to respond appropriately to those around them. That is what happened to Martin Rollins, who, following the death of one of his children, became consumed by the fear that "the world is going to hell in a handbasket." While he was able to maintain his work schedule, he would not mix with his colleagues at work. In time he began to feel that his former friends were trying to take advantage of him. The more he felt that way, the more paranoid he behaved. Mr. Rollins thought that even his closest friends were taking advantage of his vulnerability for their own gain. As time went on, he managed his tasks less and less effectively. In turn, this behavior made him feel more vulnerable and worthless. It became impossible for him to distinguish whether his fears were based on reality or on illusion.

The sad fact is that many mourners *are* taken advantage of, wittingly or unwittingly, by those who see an opportunity for gain. There are those who, no matter what motives they profess, deliberately manipulate people who are vulnerable. This manipulation can take the form of encouraging them to buy impulsively, spend their money recklessly, and make decisions thoughtlessly. There are even more people who unwittingly take advantage of the vulnerable by responding to mourners' needs with clichés or by urging mourners to indulge in unhealthy practices such as drinking too much alcohol.

Despair is expressed in this poem written by a woman who hoped her words would warn others:

A Plea to Bereaved Parents

It was years ago
the night my baby died.
Didn't see him
    hold him,
    kiss him,
or say "goodbye."
People asked
How am I? "Oh, fine."
How are you feeling? "Oh, great."
So I take a little drink—
    helps me sleep.
The grief takes hold of me—
    guess one more drink won't hurt.
Nightmares come—
    more drinking.
Sweet oblivion!
Tired of pretending that all is well—
I'm over it—coping with it—
    See the smile on my face!

But the grief is still there,
It's hiding in a bottle.
They say, "It was all for the best. Lucky you didn't take
the baby home, you didn't even know it."
I reach for my friend,
    my companion,
    my confidant,
    my brandy.
"Oh, I'm fine."
Pills this time.
No harm done; it'll help me forget.
But I don't forget.
When does the living come again? I am slowly dying.
Wander down in the basement.
Why is it hard to walk?
Where is that blood coming from?
I drop my bottle—it crashes to the floor.
I drop the knife—it mixes with the blood.
The doctors said, "Suppressed feelings coming out,"
they are right.
No more drinking because I feel sick all of the time.
So the depression takes over
    weight loss
    crying spells
    confusion.
Alcoholic depression.
Big words to grasp.
Who cares? Not me.
My time is running out.
Next time I will not fail—
I will die.

The author of the poem ended with this plea to bereaved parents: "Don't hide your grief. Don't drink your grief away; it doesn't work. Deal with it. Face it. Cry. Scream. Yell. You have the right. I am wondering how many bereaved parents reading this have succumbed to alcohol as a way to fight or bury their grief as I did? It started with losing my baby, and then *all* other problems I faced with a drink. Be careful. It's a one-way ticket to hell."

Seeking the Help of Others

To avoid the derelict, sick, or despairing roles, a mourner needs the support of others. Support from family and friends can help mourners sort through those things truly needing to be done and identify those things that realistically can be accomplished. On the other hand, mourners need encouragement through the presence of others to exert what energy they do have to take care of survival needs. Mourners must maintain daily rituals of hygiene and nutrition, no matter how bad they feel.

Few people enjoy eating alone. Friends and relatives need to understand the importance of eating in a social setting. Straightforwardness is important not only so that others can know your needs, but so that you can consciously work within your limits. Others cannot be mind readers. You need to be explicit with them. You may need help, for instance, in planning simple menus or organizing the tasks of daily living.

One woman complained that she could not remember whether she had taken her blood-pressure medicine until one of her friends gave her a pill box divided into seven compartments—one for each day of the week. That friend came to her home weekly to visit and to remind her to organize her medications for the week.

Another mourner reported that he could not find things such as his checkbook, other important documents, his reading glasses, and his keys to the car. With the help of a friend he organized one spot in the house where he kept everything that he needed for regular living. "Even though that place looked like a trash heap," he said, "I knew I could find everything I needed there."

You may also need others to help you maintain your spiritual rituals. At times of heightened disorientation, prayers that are only private can become more alienating and may leave you feeling more in despair. Prayers that are both personal and part of corporate worship remind you that you are not alone. Even more important is involvement in religious rituals that help you keep your perspective and see yourself as part of a specific people at a definite place in a given time— all necessary components for orientation.

The disorganization faced by mourners who have experienced the loss of a loved one is likely to be the most intense disorientation of their lives. It is comforting to know, though, that the overwhelming majority do recover and discover that out of this experience comes the radical reassessment necessary for new life.

8

When Mourning
Is Almost Over

"Will I get over my grief?" That must
be the question most frequently
asked by mourners as the long days and longer nights drag
on beyond what even the most experienced have expected.
If you are asking a similar question and you mean, "Will I
ever forget the emotional pain of my loss?" the answer is
"no." It is impossible to forget those whom we have loved
and difficult to repress the feelings of suffering which have
been so much a part of mourning. If your question, however,
is, "Will I ever be able to get on with other aspects of my
life?" the answer is "yes." Many mourners report that while
feelings of grief overcome them from time-to-time, particularly on anniversaries and holidays, the intensity of the pain
and the duration of disorientation become less severe.

Experiencing Reorganization

How will you know when your disorientation is about over?
There are four signs, which together constitute "reorganization." *Reorganization* refers to mourners' *adaptation* to the

77

changes forced on them by their loss and the *reorientation* of a sense of self in their new lives.

Characteristics of reorientation which dominate near the end of the second year after death of a loved one

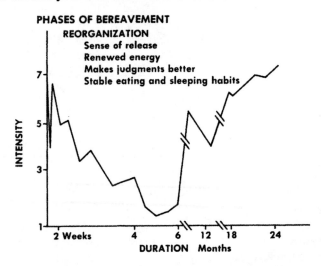

PHASES OF BEREAVEMENT

REORGANIZATION
Sense of release
Renewed energy
Makes judgments better
Stable eating and sleeping habits

INTENSITY

2 Weeks   4   6   12   18   24

DURATION   Months

The strongest sign and often the first to be realized is a *sense of release*. Instead of being obsessed with memories of the deceased, feeling lonely, or wondering what the loved ones would think were they alive, mourners begin to give attention to the challenges and opportunities for living. Erica and Warren, for example, found that they were becoming less and less concerned about revenge for the death of their son and more and more concerned with planning for the future. They discovered that they could enjoy their other children and allow themselves to become more involved with friends and family. "It was almost like the old days," Erica said, "except that every once in a while I would begin to cry unexpectedly when somewhere in the darkest recesses of my mind I would think about our missing son."

Other mourners report that they no longer found it important to continue some of the rituals of living that they had associated with memories of the deceased. They put away or even gave away some of the possessions of the deceased, reorganized living space, and engaged in social activities that were not part of the relationship before the loss. As one woman commented, "Why, I even go out dancing. My late husband would never have approved. After he died, I would have felt guilty if I had gone dancing, but now I realize the reason that he didn't approve is that he had never learned how to dance and have fun in that way."

A second sign of reorganization is *renewed energy*. After the long weeks of feeling fatigued, Marge reported that one bright spring morning she felt like she could dig up the garden space and start planting flowers. She reported that that burst of energy was rather dramatic. Some people do have rather dramatic recoveries of energy, usually coming after the first anniversary, but most mourners discover that they have adapted to the loss of their loved one by far more subtle signs. Linda, for example, indicated that it was all that she could do to get the meals ready for the family, get the children off to school, and take care of herself. She reported that she had no energy left for doing anything else. After the anniversary of the loss of her baby, though, she found that she had a higher energy level and was able to return to some of her volunteer activities. By the time the second anniversary of her loss came around, she was feeling ready for a new pregnancy.

A third sign of reorganization is *making better judgments*. This sign is sometimes misread, because many mourners feel that they have rebounded quickly and are making the same quality of decision that they had prior to their crisis. One study in which parents were asked how soon they recovered from the loss of their child found that most of the parents thought they were pretty well back to "normal" in about six weeks after their loss, at least in making their own judgments. They did not realize that a long period of disorganization was still ahead of them.

By interviewing employers, friends, and relatives of mourners, I have found that it takes much longer to return to a qualitative level of making decisions than many mourners have assumed. Making qualitative judgments requires the ability to concentrate. People do not concentrate well until they have worked through the obsessions that are associated with the deceased. This is not to say that mourners are unable to make decisions, but rather that they are not able to follow through on decisions or to make decisions with the same efficiency. Most mourners report a great deal of procrastination about making decisions. Warren, the insurance executive, reported that about 18 months after he had lost his son, he recovered his ability to concentrate and in a matter of days had moved the piles of paper off of his desk.

A fourth sign of reorganization is a *return to stable eating habits and to precrisis sleeping habits.* When both weight and sleeping habits are stabilized, mourners have adapted to the consequences of change in their lives.

For an adult it seems to take between 18 and 24 months before these four signs become dominant. It takes about two years to adapt to major changes in life, whether those changes are positive or negative.

Through hindsight, many mourners discover that the signs of reorganization began to appear as soon as they did one of several things: anticipated loss, cared for the loved one, finished both economic and psychological "business" with the dying person, or arranged the funeral. Each of these involves completing a part of life. Questions such as: "Why me?" "Why did this happen?" "Did I do everything I should?" reveal a searching for and sorting through values to set priorities. Pausing in activities, reassessing daily routines and habits, and distinguishing feelings are part of the work of shifting from the past to the future.

Telling Your Story on Anniversaries

Anniversaries are a time to remember. Birthdays mark beginnings in life. Marriage anniversaries call back memories not only of the day that vows of commitment were exchanged publicly but also those times of laughs and tears that marked the coming together of two persons' affections. Anniversaries of death also recall memories. In Jewish tradition a special memorial service is held during the festivals of the Day of Atonement for the purpose of mourning those who have died and giving thanks for their lives. The service is a public opportunity to express ongoing bonds of attachment by sharing memories of the deceased.

Many countries have occasions for recalling the deceased, particularly those who gave their lives for the defense of their country. Memorial Day is one such occasion in the United States and is met with mixed reactions. Some people, particularly those in service organizations and churches, take special note. Most people, however, try to escape the day's meaning and turn the occasion into a vacation or holiday. The mixed reaction is symbolic of the uncertainty North Americans have about the place of mourning. Even some pastors are known to condemn mourners' feelings of remorse, and they make no liturgical provisions for marking the occasion—not unlike physicians who want their patients to suppress grief with medications. Some rationalize their positions by quoting Jesus' command to his disciples: "Leave the dead to bury their own dead," apparently forgetting that Jesus gave the command, "but as for you, go and proclaim the kingdom of God" (Luke 9:60).

The major challenge for most mourners is how to get beyond the dread of anniversaries. Organizing specific activities for these occasions seems to be the most effective way to do this.

Most religions have developed liturgies which recall for their members the debt each generation owes its predecessors and the obligation that the present generation has for passing its heritage to succeeding generations. The liturgies give mourners permission to express their feelings and to have their feelings acknowledged publicly. In the telling of the stories of the tradition, individuals are given permission to add their personal story to the tradition.

What should you do in anticipation of the anniversary of your loss? Plan ahead. Arrange some special public service by which you can acknowledge your loss. Place flowers at your place of worship or in a hospital or nursing home. Prepare food for relatives, friends, or the needy. Invite your closest friends and relatives to join you for part of the day. Give them clear messages about what you feel would be appropriate. Be explicit about your feelings and desires.

Some groups, like mutual-help groups for mourners, arrange special services for prayer, meditation, and comfort; they send cards or phone words of support; they arrange for a meal and visitation on anniversaries.

Telling Your Story on Holidays

Holidays are also times of remembering, especially those that recall memories of fun and laughter. Many mourners report that their first Christmas, New Year's Day, or Easter became the hardest day to endure. The contrast between tinsel and glitter and how they really felt was overwhelming. The emptiness, pain, and disorientation left many feeling that they could not feel at all.

It is important to remember that your abilities to cope are compromised and your levels of energy are limited. You do not function as well when your endurance is reduced. Your major task is to set realistic limits for yourself. What is most important and meaningful for you and your family? Set those priorities with family and friends *ahead* of the coming holiday.

The Fox Valley, Illinois, chapter of the Compassionate Friends organized the following inventory to help mourners at Christmas. This inventory can also be applied to other holidays:

1. We must decide what we can handle comfortably and let these needs be known to family, friends, and relatives: whether to talk about our loved one openly; whether we can handle responsibility for things such as the family dinner, holiday

parties, etc., or whether someone else should be responsible this year; whether to stay at home for the holidays, or choose to "run away" to a totally different environment this year.

2. We must not be afraid to make changes. It can make things much less painful: open presents Christmas Eve instead of Christmas morning; have dinner at a different time; attend a different church for the Christmas Eve service; let the children take over tree decorating, making cookies, etc.

3. Our greatest comfort may come in doing something for others. Some mourners feel they can acknowledge their loss more meaningfully by: giving a gift in memory of their loved one; donating money they would have spent on that person's gift to a favorite charity; adopting a needy family for the holidays; inviting a guest (such as a foreign student or senior citizen) to share the festivities.

4. Whether the subject is greeting cards, holiday baking, putting up the tree, or decorating outside, we need to ask: Have I involved or considered all my family? Do I *really enjoy* doing this? Do *other* family members really enjoy doing this? Is this a task that can be shared by other family members? Would Christmas be Christmas without it?

5. How many stockings shall we hang? We may decide to put them all up, hang no stockings at all, or put thoughts and feelings about our loved one on notes to be placed in that special stocking. Family members should be free to read these (a special opportunity for younger children to express feelings). One family burns a special candle in memory of their absent daughter. One mother buys a poinsettia for her home as a living memorial to her son for the holiday season. Another always orders a bouquet of orange daisies. Christmas shopping is easier if you make the entire list out ahead of time. Then, when you have a "good day," you can do all your shopping at once. If the thought of sending holiday cards is too exhausting, but some of your friends don't know your loved one has died, enclose a funeral service card inside the purchased greeting cards. Take one day at a time. Be realistic. Recognize that we need to set limits to do those things which are meaningful to ourselves and our families. Know that

whatever you choose to do this year, you may decide to handle it differently next year. Growth and change go hand in hand. And don't forget that comforting discovery that many mourners confirmed: when that "special day" arrives, it's truly not as bad as we anticipated.

Preparing an inventory ahead of time will help you channel your feelings usefully. By including friends, family, and those you turn to for counsel, you are helping both yourself and them to develop realistic expectations. Preparation of an inventory is one constructive way for you to tell your story.

Anniversaries and special days may continue to be disruptive and disorienting to family and social life. Their celebrations are reminiscent of earlier times and consequently challenge you to reexamine priorities of the present. As adaptation continues, however, the intensity and duration of disorientation on these days will be decreased.

The point at which mourners have completed their reorganization is not easily measured. Yet a new reorientation will bring the insight that despite the loss of a loved one, strength was found to bear inevitable difficulties and disappointments with a sense of dignity. It is this point, in the words of Rose Kennedy, "of knowing that tragedies befall everyone, and that, although one may seem singled out for special sorrow, worse things have happened many times to others in the world, and it is not tears but determination that makes pain bearable."[1] Tears are the lubricant for making transitions, but determination is what enables individuals to reestablish patterns of meaningful activity. Mourning is a process necessary for finding that road to the future. Shortcuts that may be used to make the process shorter, to suppress its characteristics, or to ignore its consequences are futile because these same shortcuts often cause further disorientation.

9

Models for
Helping Mourners

You may be one of many persons who
have never experienced the loss of
someone close, or, if you have, you may still feel unable to
cope with your disorientation. One of the inappropriate ways
of handling loss is to allow someone else to take over your
day-to-day responsibilities, leaving you passively engaged
with living. The best way of handling your disorientation to
loss is to be around those who, as fellow mourners—past or
present—can serve as models for reorientation and problem
solving.

Models for mourners are persons who, in the course of their
own living, provide cues or ways which reorient mourners
for their own actions and problem solving. When Clara Wilson was widowed, she thought she wanted to flee all responsibilities—not only for her husband's estate, but also for
her own well-being. Her oldest sister had always been "the
take-charge person" in the family and did just that when Mrs.
Wilson called to say her husband had just died. No detail was
too small for the sister's attention. In sparing Mrs. Wilson her
grief, the sister made all the decisions about the funeral, about

settlement of the estate, the immediate sale of Mrs. Wilson's home and consequent move into a highrise apartment, and Mrs. Wilson's supposed needs for tranquilizing medications. Mrs. Wilson herself made few, if any, decisions for several months. When Mrs. Wilson failed after several months to begin taking some initiative, the sister became alarmed by the thought that she would have her as a ward for the indefinite future. She demanded that Mrs. Wilson see a psychiatrist.

With the help of therapy, Mrs. Wilson discovered how her refusal to accept responsibility was a state of chronic anger at her husband for leaving her and also that such behavior was the worst way to live. She had agreed with few of the decisions her sister had made. The more she had disagreed with her sister, the more angry and passive Mrs. Wilson had become. Until she learned to channel her anger more appropriately, Mrs. Wilson had become more and more disoriented.

Concurrent with her therapy, Mrs. Wilson began to attend a mutual-help group for mourners. Members of the group listened to her and encouraged her to articulate and analyze her problems realistically. They did not allow her to pass her responsibilities on to someone else, however. They shared with her their successes and failures in solving their own problems. What Mrs. Wilson learned is that even though she was confused about her life, it was only as she worked at reorienting herself that she could discover what to do and how to do it. It took others to show her the real from the fictional in her confusion and anger. Mutual-help groups for mourners not only provide access to models of reoriented and functioning persons, but they provide talent and expertise for solving the unique problems of loss.

Hospice Bereavement Support Service

The people in the three case illustrations with which this book began were disoriented about themselves following the death of their loved one. Marge, the widow who had cared for her husband through a long, debilitating illness, turned for help to the hospice in her community.

In more than 2000 communities in North America, hospices provide help for those who are dying. While hospice staff members are available primarily to help patients, they are trained in a philosophy that recognizes the close relationship between patients and their families. As a consequence, many hospices have an established network of volunteers to help mourners. Many of the volunteers are former mourners themselves.

When Marge and her husband knew that he was dying, they were referred to the nearest hospice. After assessment of the husband's disease and prognosis, the hospice director outlined the kinds of services available. Marge wanted to care for her husband at home. The hospice staff helped her locate equipment such as a high movable bed, bedpan, and feeding devices. The hospice physician reviewed medical needs and helped the patient find appropriate drug levels for controlling pain. The hospice home-care nurse made regular visits to monitor their needs. As important as this assistance was, Marge found that the greatest help came from the hospice volunteers. They took turns at the bedside so Marge could get some rest or get away from her home on occasion. Volunteers helped with such chores as buying groceries and filling prescriptions. They also helped Marge by directing her to reliable advisors—legal, financial, and business.

After her husband's death, Marge was phoned or visited by the same hospice volunteers who checked to make sure she was coping appropriately. They provided a network of continuing support for her through her major crises. "They never told me what to do or not to do," Marge relates, "but they helped me think out loud what I needed to do, and that kept me from making lots of mistakes. You know, when you're left alone you can often feel like going crazy!"

Hospice volunteers provide models for mourners by the activities of caring. They are not counselors and do not present themselves as such, though they know how, if needed, to refer a mourner to professional counselors in the hospice network. They remind us that much of the work of adapting to loss is coping with the day-by-day chores of living.

The Compassionate Friends

When Erica and Warren lost their son, they didn't know where to turn. "It just seemed that all of our friends felt as helpless as we did," Warren confided. "Our usual ways of handling problems didn't work." Their pastor recommended that they investigate a mutual-help group which focuses on the needs of people who have lost children of any age. Erica had heard of a group and was receptive to the idea, but Warren said, "The last thing I needed was to spill my guts for a bunch of strangers." Yet when Warren did go, he not only "spilled his guts" emotionally, but found those strangers supportive as he began to use emotions to clarify his sense of reality rather than using his energies to suppress emotions and perpetuate confusion. The group helped Warren find ways of expressing his own sorrow and also to be sensitive to Erica's emotional needs. He concluded: "Most importantly, they helped me figure out how to relate to our friends again."

Members of Compassionate Friends chapters are bereaved parents. Their motto is that couples like Erica and Warren "need not walk alone" in their sorrow. Most chapters meet monthly to discuss such problems as how to accept death or how to handle holidays after the death of a child. Members provide a support network for mourners who find that they either do not have a nurturing social group or that their families or social groups are not providing them appropriate support in their sorrow. Some individuals report that through mutual-help groups like the Compassionate Friends they have established long-term friendships. Others find their chapter friendships useful only as long as their mourning is intense. In either case, the strength of such groups is in providing emotional and intellectual support when other groups are unavailable, unsupportive, or inadequate.

SHARE

After the death of their baby, Linda and Gordon felt they had handled their disorientation fairly well. The only thing that seemed to indicate continuing problems was that Linda seemed unable to become pregnant again. She and Gordon had submitted to numerous medical procedures. Nothing could be found that would explain infertility. The obstetrician suggested that they investigate the activities of the local SHARE chapter, because their mourning may have been suppressed and that may have led to infertility.

SHARE is a mutual-help group for those who have lost a baby because of miscarriage, stillbirth, or early infant death. At the beginning of the group's meeting, the following guidelines are read:

1. Each of your experiences are unique and valid. No one is here to criticize or analyze.
2. Feel free to share your feelings and experiences. We will not probe. If you had a similar experience and care to relate to what others share, feel free to do so.
3. Note pads are available for you to write down anything which comes to mind. It is okay to write while others are talking. Notes are for yourself and you will not be asked to share them.
4. It is acceptable to cry. There are tissues available and we ask that you be sensitive to your neighbor's needs. We ask your permission to cry, too.
5. If you feel the need to leave, feel free to go. One of us will follow you out of the room to be sure that you are ready to drive before you leave.
6. Share your feelings about the meeting with your spouse. We do not want to create a communication gap, but rather to increase communication.

7. The group time is not intended as a time for medical advice. If you have medical questions, we will respond to them after the general meeting.

8. Should you wish to share a bad experience you have had with a hospital, nurse or doctor, feel free to relate the experience. We would ask that you not use the names of the institution or professionals in the discussion.

9. To respect the privacy of each parent, we will not discuss, except with SHARE members, the content of these meetings.

10. After the short presentation, you may respond to what the speaker has said or open with anything you wish to bring up. We encourage you to respond to each other.

While initially skeptical that they would find help from others, Linda and Gordon discovered that they had repressed many feelings, some they had not even shared with each other. Through the education programs and the exchanges with other couples, they found that they had denied facing a number of problems that became more pervasive after their baby died. Uncertainty about how to manage finances, how to establish realistic expectations with their parents as well as their in-laws, and how to distribute home responsibilities had all been avoided. Linda did not become pregnant exactly when she wanted, but when the baby was born, both she and her husband were better prepared.

While the purpose and focus of mutual-help groups differ, their function is basically the same: to help mourners find those ways by which they can recover their orientation and function responsibly. They provide the nurturing social network many mourners do not otherwise have.

What should you expect from a mutual-help group? You should expect a group to:

• encourage you to face the reality of your loss, calling the deceased by name and placing your loss in a specific context;

- encourage you to express your emotions honestly and to explore your questions forthrightly;
- support you to become more autonomous and less dependent on those who shelter you in your grief;
- guide you to competent advisors—financial, medical, social, emotional, or spiritual;
- recommend ways for coping better with your own feelings and with your relationships to others; and
- challenge you to look at life beyond your loss.

Some groups may fail you. If you do not find your group helping you become more oriented to your world, then you may leave the group without apology. Sometimes either a professionally trained or lay volunteer facilitator of a group can be controlling and manipulating, actually trying to work out their own problems through yours. If you feel yourself being manipulated, becoming more rather than less dependent, being pressured to do what you feel is inappropriate, then that group is not for you. Fortunately, most mutual-help groups avoid such failures. For mourners, the probable benefits far outweigh the risks.

10

Mourning Becomes Compassion

Mourning is a universal experience that is intensely disorienting and lonely, yet it is widely misunderstood by both laity and the trained professionals in North America. If mourning is acceptable behavior at all, it is assumed that it should be brief in duration—even if very intense. Unlike the mourners of the past, mourners today allow themselves only a couple of hours for the funeral or several days off at most from their regular duties.

How emotions and behaviors of mourning are expressed affect health. As much as mourners may try to deny that anything significant has happened when someone they loved dies and no matter how skilled they become in trying to mask their feelings, they still know that their deceptive behavior is a lie. How they pray that others know they lie and will reach out to them in their confusion!

Mourning is a complex set of emotions, which, if allowed to function appropriately, can help in the reorientation process. In this book I have focused on the disorientation following the death of a loved one, but equally important are other losses such as divorce, children leaving home, loss of a job or home, and change of body image. It is common to "mourn" even when change has been positive and desirable, though rapid enough to leave a feeling of disorientation. This type of mourning is often a result of a renewed awareness of time passing: graduation from college, marriage, birth of a wished-for child, a promotion, or a move to a new community. The experience may seem overwhelming.

The emotions of mourning can be frightening. Confusion, bizarre thoughts, or swings of emotions are common. Anger and tears may erupt without warning: a sense of defeat and depression may linger longer than anyone would guess. The tasks of reordering one's life may be far more difficult than imagined. No matter the clichés and words of assurance, emotions are uncontrollable at times.

Reorientation, the adaptation to loss, begins when it is possible to distinguish between frustration with personal feelings and frustration with what is causing those feelings. It is not the emotions of mourning that cause suffering, but the events that triggered those emotions.

A major step toward recovery occurs when a mourner can call emotions by name: "I'm angry," "I'm depressed," "I'm amused." At this time it is possible to analyze what precisely has stimulated the emotion. Confusion results with attempts to ignore feelings, or worse, to repress them because of an inability to look at what has stimulated them. To refuse to examine the source of disorientation is to deny a basic reality of life. The problem will continue to cause frustration unless it is resolved.

Disorientation and profound frustration occur when relationships of affection, attachment, or bonding are broken by the loss of a loved one. Even if death has been expected, the cues of the relationship which provided orientation to personhood and to the sense of place and time are disrupted in many unexpected ways. At its most profound level, mourning reveals the bedrock of faith. In the loss of another, people discover what they expected and did not question, who they trusted and did not doubt, how they assumed but did not cherish. They may discover that their faith has been in gods of their own making, now shattered.

It is little wonder that many mourners are scandalized by the depth of their anger at others—at God, the loved one who died, physicians or pastors, even themselves. I am not so concerned when mourners express anger. At least these individuals are blessed with the will to fight. Far worse are those who fall into despair and passivity. They not only lose the will to work beyond their disorientation, but give up basic rituals of survival—eating, drinking, exercising, and resting. There are those well-meaning consolers, like Job's friends, who mouth clichés: "It was God's will"; "Your child is better off dead than alive"; "He no longer suffers." Even if true, such consolation misses the point with which mourners wrestle—even if it provides comfort for the consolers. Mourners suffer because their expectations, trusts, and assumptions have been betrayed.

There are five personal attributes which seem to determine whether mourners can adapt successfully to their loss or whether mourning becomes the occasion for their own dying.

1. Understanding Basic Survival Needs

No matter what faith an individual follows, basic human needs cannot be ignored. A pious widow, in the depth of her disorientation, became so convinced of her loneliness that she refused the company of others and was so lacking in appetite that she refused to eat or drink. She rested little and exercised not at all. She kept her Bible open most of the time, prayed that the Lord would spare her the plight of suffering, and listened to religious messages. Despite her piety, she found her prayers ignored and she became increasingly enraged, especially at her friends and at God.

One day while listening to a recorded sermon in which the pastor was telling a story about himself, it occurred to her that a similar story would apply to her: What if she died and went to heaven.? What if at the heavenly gates she demanded an audience with God? What if her demand were granted and she inquired of God, "Where were you when I prayed to be spared my grief?" And what if God answered: "I sent you friends and you turned them away. I ordered Meals-on-Wheels to come daily, and you ate and drank nothing. Neither would you stretch nor rest; yet I provided you all you needed!" What the widow called her faith was nothing more than her anger turned on herself, and she was choosing to punish herself by ignoring her survival needs.

2. A Sense of Personal Esteem

Mourners with self-esteem have personal hopes and aspirations for living, as well as fears of loneliness, suffering and death. Instead of fleeing life's problems, they work to distinguish between their responsibilities and what cannot be avoided.

3. Ability to Relate to Others

Relational skills must be developed and practiced in order to be maintained. Inability to resolve frustrations, to process conflict, or to handle affection make it dubious that a mourner will have a nurturing support network of other human beings. Without others, people become slaves to their own suspicions and become chronically disoriented. With others, personal suspicions can be tested and brought under control. Reality can be identified and analyzed.

4. The Desire to Improve Coping Skills and Deepen One's Understanding of Life

Only a masochist wills to suffer. The healthy-minded have stopped denying the unwanted change in their lives and want to make something constructive out of their experiences.

Some mourners speak of how they learned to care for themselves and consequently now care for others as they seldom did before their crisis. They speak of how they learned to forgive themselves and as a result can now forgive others. Others tell about how they arrived at a mature religion that freed them of much magical thinking and provided them a faith for living. One man spoke of how his crisis of loss forced him to give up habits of pouting, well-learned in childhood, when he discovered his deceased mother would not come to rescue him. He reported: "Until then, I wanted to die. Now I can go on living. I have found friends, I have found a new vocation."

5. Improved Understanding

A fifth attribute of mourners who have successfully adapted to loss is improved understanding of how human beings function, feel, and take meaning from life. Rather than accepting only what others have told them, mourners who have adapted to loss used their own experiences to question, explore, and resolve conflicts forced on them in their loss. They learned to allow their feelings to alert them and identify personal limits that need respect.

It is not by magic that mourners become reoriented. While much depends on courage and determination, even maintaining basic survival needs are gifts. The ways parents and teachers prepare their young for facing the realities of living, the many ways others seek to reach out for comfort, the many people responsible for availability of food and drink—all are part of the mystery of compassion.

Compassion means to risk entering into another's suffering. To become involved in another's suffering is risky, because their problems may become one's own. Their disorientation may overwhelm one's own sense of stability and detract from one's personal priorities. The paradox however is that the more people risk, the more unlikely they are to be intimidated by the problems that are the occasions of human suffering. It is part of the mystery of grace that in the compassion of reciprocating concern for each other, people not only become reorienters for others but their own wounds are healed.

Notes

Preface

1. John Bowlby and Colin Murray Parkes, "Separation and Loss Within the Family," in E. James Anthony and Cyrille Koupernik, eds., *The Child in His Family* (New York: Wiley, 1970).

Chapter 1

1. Thomas H. Holmes and Richard H. Rahe, "The Social Readjustment Rating Scale," *Journal of Psychosomatic Research*, 1967, 11:213-218.
2. Colin Murray Parkes, *Bereavement: Studies of Grief in Adult Life* (New York: International Universities Press, 1972).
3. James J. Lynch, *The Broken Heart: The Medical Consequences of Loneliness* (New York: Basic Books, 1977), p. 56.

Chapter 2

1. Erich Lindemann, "Symptomatology and Management of Acute Grief," *American Journal of Psychiatry*, 1944, 101:148.
2. W. Dewi Rees and Sylvia G. Lutkins, "The Mortality of Bereavement," *British Medical Journal*, 1967, 4:13-16.
3. James J. Lynch, *The Broken Heart*.
4. Helen F. Dunbar, *Emotions and Bodily Changes*, 4th ed. (New York: Columbia University Press, 1954).
5. Richard Dayringer, Glen W. Davidson, Rosalia E. A. Paiva, and Nancy Pistorius, "Ethical Issues in the Practice of Medicine: A 1980 Study of the Behavior and Opinions of 800 Illinois Physicians," *Department of Medical Humanities Report 81/1* (Springfield: Southern Illinois University School of Medicine, 1981).

6. R. W. Bartrop, E. Luckhurst, L. Zazarus, and L. G. Kiloh, "Depressed Lymphocyte Function After Bereavement" *The Lancet*, 1977, 1:834-839; Steven J. Schleifer, Steven E. Keller, Maria Camerino, John C. Thornton, and Marvin Stein, "Suppression of Lymphocyte Stimulation Following Bereavement" *Journal of The American Medical Association*, 1983, 250:374-377.

7. Lisa F. Berkman and Lester Breslow, *Health and Ways of Living* (New York: Oxford University Press, 1983).

8. William R. Beisel, Robert Edelman, Kathleen Nauss, and Robert M. Suskind, "Single-Nutrient Effects on Immunologic Functions." *Journal of The American Medical Association*, 1981, 245:53-58.

9. Carol West Suiter and Merrily Forbes Hunter, *Nutrition: Principles and Applications in Health Promotion* (Philadelphia: J. B. Lippincott, 1980), p. 14.

10. Charles F. Ehret, K. R. Groh, and J. C. Meinert, "Circadian Dischronism and Chronotypic Ecophilia as Factors in Aging and Longevity," in *Aging and Biological Rhythm*, Harvey V. Sarnis Jr. and Salvatore Capobianco, eds. (New York: Plenum Publishing Co., 1978).

Chapter 3

1. John Bowlby, "Pathological Mourning and Childhood Mourning," *Journal of the American Psychoanalytic Association*, 1963, 11:500-541; Colin Murray Parkes, "Determination of Outcome Following Bereavement" *Proceedings of the Royal Society of Medicine*, 1971, 64:279.

2. J. William Worden, *Grief Counseling and Grief Therapy* (New York: Springer Publishing Co., 1982).

3. Glen W. Davidson, *Understanding Death of a Wished-for Child* (Springfield, IL: OGR Service Corp., 1979).

Chapter 4

1. Arnold van Gennep, *The Rites of Passage* (Chicago: University of Chicago Press, 1960).

2. R. C. Satzberger, "Death: Beliefs, Activities and Reactions of the Bereaved: Some Psychological and Anthropological Observations," in *The Human Context*, Rudolph Moose, ed., (New York: Wiley, 1975), pp. 103-116.

3. H. Richard Niebuhr, *Radical Monotheism and Western Culture* (New York: Harper and Brothers, 1960).

Chapter 6

1. Karl Menninger, *Whatever Became of Sin?* (New York: Hawthorn Books, 1973).

Chapter 7

1. E. H. Volkart, "Bereavement and Mental Health," in *Explorations in Social Psychiatry*, A. J. Leighton, J. A. Clausen, and R. N. Wilson, eds. (New York: Basic Books, 1957).
2. Thomas H. Holmes, and Richard H. Rahe, "The Social Readjustment Rating Scale," *Journal of Psychosomatic Research*, 1967, 11:213-218.
3. George W. Brown and J. L. T. Birleyu, "Crises and Life Changes and the Onset of Schizophrenia." *Journal of Health and Social Behavior*, 1968, 9:203-214; Eugene S. Paykel, Brigette A. Prusoff, and E. H. Uhlenhuth, "Scaling of Life Events." *Archives of General Psychiatry*, 1971, 25:340-347; William G. Smith, "Critical Life Events and Prevention Strategies in Mental Health," *Archives of General Psychiatry*, 25:103-109; Jerome K. Myers, Jacob J. Lindenthal, Max P. Pepper, and David R. Ostrander, "Life Events and Mental Status: A Longitudinal Study," *Journal of Health and Social Behavior*, 1972, 13:398-406.
4. Irwin Gerber, Alfred Wiener, Delia Battin, and Arthur M. Arkin, "Brief Therapy to the Aged Bereaved," in Bernard Schoenberg, et al., eds., *Bereavement: Its Psychosocial Aspects* (New York: Columbia University Press, 1975).

Chapter 8

1. Cleveland Amory, "When Faith Is Triumphant: A Portrait of Rose Fitzgerald Kennedy," *Parade Magazine*, July 3, 1983, p.4.

For Further Reading

Berezin, Nancy. *After a Loss in Pregnancy: Help for Families Affected by a Miscarriage, a Still Birth, or a Newborn's Death*. New York: Simon and Schuster, 1982.

This book helps parents who have suffered the death of a child before or at birth understand the best of current medical knowledge about obstetrical risks and intensive infant care. A particularly helpful chapter is entitled "Children: The Forgotten Mourners."

Clinebell, Howard. *Growth Counseling: Hope-Centered Methods of Actualizing Human Wholeness*. Nashville: Abingdon, 1979.

A description of the principle, the methods, and the theological basis for counseling that focuses on a person's positive potential rather than on their failures and weaknesses.

Davidson, Glen W., ed. *Hospice: Development and Administration* (2nd ed.). Washington, D.C.: Hemisphere; New York: McGraw Hill, 1984.

A group of clinicians and researchers look at the greatest citizen-initiated change in the history of North American health care delivery. Chapters include how to organize and manage a hospice; how best to support the emotional needs of the bereaved, including a Protestant-Catholic-Jewish liturgical response; and prominent ethical and legal issues of palliative care. An extensive, annotated bibliography is included.

DeSpelder, Lynne Ann, and Strickland, Albert Lee. *The Last Dance: Encountering Death and Dying*. Palo Alto, CA: Mayfield Publishing Co., 1983.

A richly illustrated textbook in which the authors discuss the theoretical, practical, and personal issues of dying and death. An extensive chapter is included on death in children's lives.

Lieberman, Morton A.; Borman, Leonard D.; and Associates. *Self-Help Groups for Coping with Crisis*. San Francisco: Jossey-Bass, Inc., 1979.

Scholars look at the nature of the self-help group movement in North America. Chapters are organized under these four categories: how groups are started and structured, who participates in self-help groups, how self-help groups work, and evaluating the impact of self-help groups.

Nouwen, Henri J. *In Memoriam*. Notre Dame, IN: Ave Maria Press, 1980.

A Roman Catholic priest writes a letter to friends telling them about the death of his mother. The letter is realistic and insightful, as the author gives a refreshing re-examination of death from the Christian perspective.

Nouwen, Henri J. *A Letter of Consolation*. San Francisco: Harper & Row, 1982.

The letter the author wrote to his father six months after the death of his mother.

Parkes, Colin Murray, and Stevenson-Hinde, Joan, eds. *The Place of Attachment in Human Behavior*. New York: Basic Books, Inc., 1982.

Eighteen internationally renowned researchers and clinicians trace the crucial role of attachment and bonding in the evolution of human personality throughout the life cycle. The authors show how loss—the breaking of affectional bonds—leads to disorientation, and for some mourners, psychopathology.

Wass, Hennelore, ed. *Dying: Facing the Facts*. Washington, D.C.: Hemisphere; New York: McGraw-Hill, 1979.

Written for those who need facts in order to cope with loss and anxiety about death. Part One explores attitudes and behaviors that emphasize the complexity of attitudes toward death in society. Part Two covers known facts such as the physiology, psychology, and sociology of dying. Part Three focuses on the challenges and issues, both technical and ethical, involved with ways people face dying.

Worden, J. William. *Grief Counseling and Grief Therapy: A Handbook for the Mental Health Practitioner*. New York: Springer Publishing Co., 1982.

Although this is written for the mental-health professional, mourners will find this a readable text that can provide the means by which to assess whether a counselor or therapist is competent for treating grief-related problems.

Directory of Organizations

Having read this book, you may wish to locate others who have had similar experiences of loss as you. The following 11 organizations have been chosen because they are among the largest mutual-help groups for the bereaved. Through their offices you can locate an appropriate group near you, obtain lists of available educational materials, and names of professionals trained to meet the special needs of mourners.

The Self-Help Center
1600 Dodge Avenue, Suite S-122
Evanston, IL 60204
(312) 328-0470

Founded by Dr. Leonard D. Borman, the Center serves as a clearing house for self- and mutual-help groups. The center's staff have found that there are groups now for sufferers of all the 17 disease categories recognized by the World Health Organization. The center is particularly helpful for locating the appropriate group nearest you.

AMEND
4324 Berrywick Terrace
St. Louis, MO 63128
(314) 487-7582

AMEND (Aiding A Mother Experiencing Neonatal Death) began as an offshoot of Lifeseekers, a voluntary organization that provided lifesaving equipment to hospitals. Trained lay counselors, many of whom have experienced the loss of a child, offer support by phone or personal visit.

Candlelighters
   2025 Eye St. NW
   Suite 1011
   Washington, D.C. 20006
   (202) 659-5136

An international organization of parents whose children have cancer or have died from the disease. "Candlelighters parents share the shock of diagnosis, the questions about treatment, the anxiety of waiting, the despair of loss, the hope of remission, and joy of cure."

The Compassionate Friends, Inc.
   P.O. Box 1347
   Oak Brook, IL 60521
   (312) 323-5010

A support group for bereaved parents, Compassionate Friends has the motto, "You need not walk alone. We are . . . people who care and share and listen to each other." The national office has available a wide range of literature and other information.

The National SIDS (Sudden Infant Death Syndrome) Foundation
   2 Metro Plaza, Suite 205
   8420 Professional Place
   Landover, MD 20785
   (301) 459-3388

The national office supports community chapters for parents who have lost children to SIDS or SIDS-related symptoms. Films, training support materials and parent-to-parent contact referral services are also provided.

The National Hospice Organization
1901 N. Fort Myers Drive, Suite 402
Arlington, VA 22209
(703) 243-5900

Hospice is a concept of care for those who are dying. More than 2000 hospices now are organized in North America. Most hospices are not-for-profit, community-based organizations of volunteers, lay persons, and professionals who have received special training in palliative care for patients and support services for families before, during, and following the death of the patient.

Parents Without Partners
7910 Woodmont Avenue, Suite 1008
Bethesda, MD 20814
(301) 654-8850

Parents Without Partners is a nonsectarian organization with over 700 chapters whose members are concerned with the welfare of single parents and their children. Their motto is "Sharing by Caring."

The Samaritans
500 Commonwealth Avenue
Boston, MA 02215
(617) 536-2460
(617) 247-0220 *for emergencies only*

The Samaritans are a special group of volunteers trained to respond to individuals considering suicide or persons who have lost a friend or relative to suicide. The emergency telephone service is covered 24 hours a day.

SHARE
St. Joseph's Health Center
300 First Capitol Drive
St. Charles, MO 63301
(314) 947-5000

Founded by Sr. Jane Marie Lamb, O.S.F., and a group of bereaved parents in Springfield, Illinois in 1977, SHARE now has over 80 chapters in nearly 30 states. The groups focus on the needs of parents who have lost a baby due to miscarriage, stillbirth, or early infant death. Their support system includes hospital staff as well as volunteers, most of whom are bereaved parents. Educational and organizational materials are available.

The THEOS Foundation
Office Building—Penn Hills Mall
Suite 410
Pittsburgh, PA 15235
(412) 243-4299

THEOS stands for "They Help Each Other Spiritually." It offers self-help assistance to young and middle-aged widowed persons. A monthly magazine and a variety of brochures and self-help materials are available.

The Widowed Persons Service
1909 K Street, N.W.
Room 580
Washington, D.C. 20049
(202) 728-4370

The Widowed Persons Service was formed jointly by the National Retired Teachers Association, the American Association of Retired Teachers, and Action for Independent Maturity. A telephone referral service, public-education programs for family adjustment, and financial and legal counseling services are available to bereaved individuals or groups interested in supporting the bereaved.